THE SCAM PROTECTOR

A book scammers don't want you to read

Adam

www.thescamprotector.com

Copyright © 2024 Adam Scott

All rights reserved.

CONTENTS:

1. Welcome to Scam Protector.
2. How severe is the situation?
3. Why is this book important?
4. What is a Scam?
5. Types of Scams.

   A. Government Imposter Scam:
   - a. IRS Scam.
   - b. SSN Scam.
   - c. Customs and Border Protection Scam.
   - d. Police Department Scam.
   - e. Government grant Scam.
   - f. Prevention from government imposter scams.

   B. Dating and Romance Scam:
   - a. Military Romance Scams.
   - b. Intimate activity Scams.
   - c. Fake dating sites Scams.
   - d. Code Verification Scams.

      e. Malware Scams.

      f. Photo Scams.

      g. Prevention from Romance Scams.

    C. Tech Scams:

      a. Lookalike websites Scam.

      b. pop-up Scam.

      c. Cold calling tech support Scam.

      d. BSOD Scam.

    D. Job offers Scam

    E. Lottery Scam

    F. Flight Booking Scam

    G. Social media Scam

    H. Online shopping scam.

6. The scam protection system.

7. Solution to this five-decade-old problem.

8. Join the revolution.

Acknowledgments.

About the author.

1. Welcome to Scam Protector

Thank you for embarking on a journey towards empowerment and protection. In an era dominated by digital transactions and online interactions, safeguarding yourself from the persistent threat of scams is paramount. "The Scam Protector" is not just a book; it is your shield against the ever-evolving landscape of online scams.

The digital realm is plagued by scams that target unsuspecting individuals, causing emotional distress and financial losses. "The Scam Protector" is your comprehensive guide, arming you with knowledge about the eight main categories and fifteen sub-categories of prevailing online scams and the Empowering Knowledge in this book makes you Scam-Resilient.

The online scam market siphons off billions of dollars from the American economy each year. This alarming statistic results from a critical gap in training and knowledge among citizens. Scammers exploit the trust, emotions, and lack of knowledge of victims to execute their scams. It's time to disrupt this cycle by arming yourself with the most potent weapon: Knowledge.

At the core of "Scam Protector" lies a simple yet powerful truth – knowledge is the most effective tool against scams. By delving into the insights behind these scams and mastering the techniques employed by fraudsters, you not only shield yourself but become a guardian for those around you. It is not just about protecting your hard-earned money; it is also about preserving your mental peace in a world where scams are rampant.

Why you should invest in this book?

In a survey conducted by gallup.com, 72% of American people worry constantly about identity theft scams, and 57% of American people fear Being tricked by a scammer into sending them money. The reason why millions of people are worried about online scams is because they lack information and knowledge about the shady tactics of scammers and fraudsters. This book equips you with that knowledge and introduces you to numerous examples of scams based on real-life events. With this knowledge, you can become an expert in spotting scams and you can protect yourself and the people around you from getting scammed.

> *"If you know the enemy and know yourself, you need not fear the result of a hundred battles. If you know yourself but not the enemy, for every victory gained you will also suffer a defeat. If you know neither the enemy nor yourself, you will succumb in every battle."*
>
> *— Sun Tzu, The Art of War*

By choosing "The Scam Protector," you are not just investing in a book; you are becoming part of a community committed to resilience and awareness. Together, we can dismantle the foundations of scams and build a more secure digital landscape for everyone.

Welcome to "The Scam Protector" – where knowledge empowers, scams crumble, and you take control of your financial and mental well-being.

Let the journey begin.

2. How Severe is the situation?

Not Hundreds, Not Thousands but Millions of people fall victim to online scams every year, losing billions of dollars to online scammers. The importance of this book cannot be overstated, especially in light of the shocking statistics revealed by the FBI in their 2022 report. A staggering $10.3 billion was deceitfully taken from hardworking individuals across the United States. This wasn't the government's money, nor was it the banks'; it was the earnings of everyday people – money painstakingly saved for significant life events like their children's weddings or their well-deserved retirements.

This massive loss could have been prevented if millions of individuals were equipped with the knowledge to defend themselves against online scams and Ponzi schemes. It's not just about the financial impact; it is also about the emotional distress, the consequences of losing one's life savings, and the erosion of trust in others and oneself. Heart-wrenching stories of individuals resorting to suicide after falling victim to scams underscore the severity of the situation.

The provided links offer a grim reality check. The FBI report link [http://tiny.cc/dy7tvz] sheds light on the alarming scale of financial deception.

Furthermore, tragic incidents, such as 20 minors taking their own lives due to an online sextortion scam [http://tiny.cc/rtptvz].

An 82-year-old grandmother committed suicide after falling prey to a lottery scam [http://tiny.cc/htptvz].

a Tennessee man ended his life following a love scam [http://tiny.cc/fiqtvz], underscoring the profound impact scams have on individuals' lives.

This book is vital as it aims not only to educate individuals on recognizing and avoiding scams but also to provide them with the tools to protect their hard-earned money and, most importantly, their well-being. By spreading awareness and empowering people with the knowledge to navigate the digital landscape safely, we can strive to prevent such devastating consequences and build a more resilient society.

I have created this book with one clear objective:

"To equip all my readers with the knowledge to detect and Eliminate any kind of scam attempt made on them"

3. Why this book is Important?

This book stands as an indispensable guide in the era where the evolution of technology has given rise to increasingly sophisticated frauds. The roots of technology-enabled fraud trace back to the 1970s, coinciding with the rise of the internet. Since then, the landscape of fraud has continually evolved, with perpetrators leveraging technology as a powerful tool to exploit innocent people.

The concerning trend of escalating fraud cases year by year can be attributed to a critical factor: the lack of upskilling among the general populace. People are falling victim to scams because of three main reasons:

- Lack of knowledge about the evolving digital landscape.
- Lack of knowledge about the right channels of information.
- Lack of training in recognizing and reporting fraud.

The absence of education and skill training has made them vulnerable targets for cunning scammers, leading to an alarming increase in online scams annually.

This groundbreaking book addresses these critical gaps by providing readers with comprehensive insights into the methodologies employed by fraudsters. Unlike any other resource, it goes beyond merely protecting individuals and their finances – it empowers them to take an active role in combating fraud at a global level. By imparting knowledge on the inner workings of scam organizations, the tools utilized in con operations, the psychology driving scammers, and the motivations behind their actions, this book equips readers with the tools needed to break free from the billion-dollar con circus.

Readers will gain a profound understanding of different scam types, allowing them to identify and protect themselves from potential threats in the future. In essence, this book serves as a digital self-defense manual, fostering digital resilience and empowering individuals to safeguard their hard-earned money from the clutches of scammers.

By arming readers with the knowledge and skills to combat fraud, this book aspires to create a movement that transcends individuals, aiming to collectively bring an end to the pervasive issue of online scams. It's not just a book; it's a call to action, inviting readers to be part of a community committed to digital self-defense and the eradication of fraudulent activities on a global scale.

4. What is a Scam?

To protect ourselves we must first know what we are protecting us from. If we go by Google's definition: "it is a dishonest scheme". A five-word definition of a four-letter word that has conned millions of people resulting in billions of dollars in losses, has forced people to commit suicide and destroyed relationships.

How can a scheme created by one individual or a group of individuals be so powerful?

What do these people do to you that you end up giving all your money to them?

The answer lies in your emotions. Every good scammer is an expert in triggering two of the most powerful emotions in human behavior which are fear and greed. Though greed is not a defined emotion it is a concept that has motivated humankind for a very long time. Once one of these triggers is activated in the human brain a huge temperament shift takes place which gives a lot of control to the scammer, and that shift is that the victim instead of understanding things starts feeling things. It switches off the rational mind of the victim and leads him to make irrational decisions.

A scam can take many forms and shapes. Execution of a scam may require various resources and technologies which may change over time but the core principle of a scam will always remain the same which is a strong trigger of fear or greed. These triggers combined with a lack of knowledge of a particular matter may make you a puppet of a scammer running around the city transferring all your hard-earned money to an unknown bank account just because a voice on the phone said so.

Scam victims not only suffer from financial losses but also lose self-respect and are left with a lifelong scar of how someone fooled them over a phone with a bunch of words supporting a scheme and they believed it.

Apart from these two emotions, the third thing a scammer will use is TRUST and URGENCY. They will always use names of reputed companies like Microsoft and Amazon, or government organizations like the IRS and SSA to gain your trust in the shortest period. Once they accomplish that, they will quickly create urgency. If you get time to think, their scheme will fail. So, they will always want you to act immediately, not giving you time to form an opinion or ask for help from an expert.

Once the first three parameters are secured next thing, they will use is SECRECY. If you go on a spree telling people what exactly is happening those people may not get triggered with the same emotion of fear and greed, their suggestions to you at that moment may ruin the scammer's plan once and for all. So, they will always tell you to not disclose the matters to anybody else till the time they get the money.

One of the last important things that will be included in Ponzi schemes or scams is loopholes. No system is perfect. There are loopholes in every system that become holy grails for conmen and they use it for their benefits. After analyzing hundreds of scam scenarios, I can tell you that most online scams work on a pattern which is:

Trust->Trigger->Urgency->Secrecy->loopholes

As we move further in this book, I will explain to you in detail how these techniques are used in different kinds of scams, and once you understand them you will be in a much better position to identify and eliminate any kind of scam attempt made on you or your family. With the knowledge and real-life examples provided in this book, you will become an expert in detecting and eliminating scams. So let us begin this revolution by understanding different kinds of scams in the next chapter.

5. Types of scams.

A. Government imposter Scams:

Scammers are constantly coming up with new schemes to deceive innocent people and one which is becoming increasingly prevalent is the government imposter scam. These scams involve individuals impersonating government officials to defraud their victims. In this Section, we will delve into the depths of government imposter scams, exploring the different types of government imposter scams and providing tips on how to prevent falling victim to these malicious schemes.

Types of government imposter scams:

Government imposter scams can take various forms, each designed to exploit you in unique ways. Here are some common types of government imposter scams to watch out for:

I) IRS scam:

It is one of the most notorious government imposter scams which involves individuals pretending to be representatives of the Internal Revenue Service (IRS). These scammers often contact their victims via phone, claiming that the individual owes back taxes and threatening legal consequences if immediate payment is not made. They may even manipulate caller ID systems to display the IRS' official phone number, making the call appear legitimate. To understand the execution of this scam let's take an example.

Angela is a middle-aged school teacher and a single mother. She is also a law-abiding citizen who has respect for the law. On one fine evening, she was watering plants in her garden when her cell phone started ringing. When she checked the phone, "IRS" was mentioned in the caller ID. She picks up the phone and a heavy male voice with an accent starts speaking.

Ben Marshall: Hello, is this Angela Johnson?

Angela: Yes, speaking. Who is this?

Ben: This is Officer Ben Marshall from the Internal Revenue Service (IRS). I'm calling to inform you that there's a serious matter that requires your immediate attention.

Angela: IRS? What's going on? I thought I paid all my taxes.

Ben: Well, Ms. Johnson, it appears that there are discrepancies in your tax filings. Our audit has revealed that you owe a significant amount of money to the IRS.

Angela: Discrepancies? I've always been honest with my taxes. I don't think I owe anything.

Ben: According to our records, the outstanding amount is $5,000. Failure to resolve this matter will lead to legal consequences, including arrest and confiscation of your assets.

Angela: $5,000? That's a lot! I can't afford that right now. What else can I do to fix this?

Ben: I understand this is a challenging situation, Ms. Johnson. However, we can work together to resolve it but first of all please write down some important details about your case, do you have a paper and pen with you?

Angela: Yes, give me the details.

Ben: first of all, write down your case ID number, it is DC 4265. Write down my name It is Ben Marshal and I am your case concerning officer. Next write down my badge ID number, IRM 6695 and lastly write down your arrest warrant number WM56824451.

Angela: I have not done anything wrong officer, what can I do to correct this?

Ben: We can offer you a one-time settlement of $2,000 if paid immediately.

Angela: I don't have that kind of money on hand. Can I set up a payment plan instead?

Ben: I'm afraid we can't do that at the moment. This is a time-sensitive matter, and we need the payment today to avoid further legal action. If you cannot make that payment right now then we will have to take legal action against you.

Angela: I don't want any legal trouble. Okay, I'll pay the $2,000. What do I need to do?

Ben: To make the payment, you can take the help of any government-authorized store near you. Which is going to be the closest?

Angela: I am sorry but, I am not aware of any government-authorized store, where can I find one?

Ben: I will find one for you tell me the zip code in which you are in right now.

Angela: 441025.

Ben: Well as I can see, there are no government-authorized stores near you, but the good news is that there is a Walmart store close to you that can help you in this situation.

Angela: Yes, I know the Walmart, it's 10 minutes away. Should I make a payment there?

Ben: Walmart does not accept tax payments Ms. Johnson but it can help you with tax payment vouchers by which you can make payments.

Angela: what is a tax payment voucher?

Ben: I will explain you everything but first you start driving towards the Walmart and very important do not disconnect the line as this recording will be used in the courthouse as a piece of evidence. Also, note that this is a private and confidential matter and you are not supposed to share this case with any other person till you get all the paperwork in hand.

Angela: But I need to talk to my lawyer first.

Ben: If you want to talk to your lawyer then it's fine but in that situation, we will have to involve our attorney as well and this will go to the courthouse. Which means that we will have to execute your arrest warrant with immediate effect.

Angela: is there any possibility that I can discuss this with my lawyer without facing the legal consequences?

Ben: well, the best I can do for you Ms. Johnson is that once you pay your remaining taxes, I can arrange a counseling session for you with an IRS officer in person and you can call your attorney in that counseling session.

Angela: Well, that sounds good. I am heading to the Walmart now.

Ben: keep the phone line open. As I told you before we need this recording as evidence that can be submitted in the courthouse. Once you reach the parking lot of the Walmart say hello to me so that I can guide you with the payment procedure.

Angela: Alright, I am here in the parking lot.

Ben: Alright all you have to do is go inside the Walmart store and look for a Walmart money card. These can be used as tax-paying vouchers. Just pick 4 Walmart money cards from the rack and load $500 on each. That would be your total payment of $2000. Once you go to meet the IRS office with your attorney just submit the card to the officer to make your payment. Do you understand the procedure?

Angela: yes, but will they load my cards as tax-paying vouchers? because they are used for Walmart shopping.

Ben: don't worry about that, I will register the cards under your name so that you can complete your payments. Right now, if anybody asks you why you need these 4 cards just tell them that they are gifts for your children so that they can shop as they like in Walmart.

Angela (after a couple of minutes): OK, I have got the 4 cards as you asked.

Ben: Alright Angela now before you go to your nearest IRS office to make payments, I need to convert these gift cards into tax payment vouchers by registering the cards in your name. Without registration, your payment will not be accepted.

Angela: OK, how do I register them?

Ben: Scratch the back of the cards gently, and help me with the numbers.

Angela: 4852-8659-8845-9658, pin: 2565….

As she gives the numbers, she gives the scammer the authority to redeem those cards with the value of $2000. Once she gives the code, the scammers get $2000 from her but the scam does not stop there. The ask for money keeps on increasing with more bogus allegations charged on her name and that's how people lose billions of dollars every year in these kinds of scams. And that's how Angela got scammed.

II) Social Security Administration scams:

Scammers also frequently impersonate officials from the Social Security Administration. In these scams, individuals receive calls or emails stating that their Social Security number has been compromised or suspended. The scammers then proceed to request personal information or payment to resolve the issue. It is important to note that government agencies will never request sensitive information or payment over the phone or through email. Here is an example to understand the execution of this scam.

John is enjoying his breakfast watching his favorite TV show on a pleasant Saturday morning when his cell phone rings. He checks his phone and it is a private number. As he generally does not get calls from private numbers, he gets curious and picks up the phone to check who it is. As he picks up the phone a smooth voice in a rude tone starts speaking.

David: Hello, is this John Smith?

John: Yes, speaking. Who's this?

David: Hi Mr. Smith, this is officer David jones from the Social Security Administration. I'm calling to inform you about some irregularities with your Social Security Number. It's a matter of urgency, and we need to resolve this immediately.

John: Irregularities with my Social Security Number? What's going on?

David: It appears that your SSN has been used for fraudulent activities. There's a warrant out for your arrest, and we need to clear this up to avoid legal consequences.

John: Warrant? Arrest? This is the first time I've heard about this. What can I do to fix it?

David: I understand that this is concerning, but we can help you resolve it. To clear your name, you'll need to cooperate with us. First, we need to verify your identity. Can you confirm your full name and the last four digits of your Social Security Number?

John: Uh, it's John Smith, and the last four digits are 1481. What do I need to do to clear this up?

David: Thank you for verifying, Mr. Smith. Now, before we proceed further, I need to inform you that we are on a federally recorded and monitored line. To write down your case details do you have a paper and pen with you?

John: Hold on for a second, let me grab one. Ok, I am ready.

David: you can start with my name; it is David Cooper and I am your case concerning officer my badge ID is SSA88594. Next, write down your case ID number which is CZ659845. Once you have it you can write down your warrant number which is ARC555869.

John: I've never heard of such a thing. I am sure you have the wrong person.

David: Your name and socials are verified Mr. Smith and we are one hundred percent sure that we have the right person. There is an affidavit in your name Mr. Smith that needs to be read verbatim on this recorded line. So, do not interrupt me while I am reading this affidavit to you Once I am done, I will provide you a fair chance to ask questions about this.

John: Alright.

David: So, we have found some fraudulent activities associated with your Social Security Number. The investigation started when we found an abandoned car on the south border of TX. The model of the car was a 2009 TOYOTA COROLLA black color with the registration no. TX982071 and we also found some Blood and drug residues inside the car. While investigating we found that the car was rented under your Name. We also found 2 addresses registered under your name. Out of the two addresses, the second address (6201 1st Ave El Paso TX 78912) was raided by the US Marshals and they recovered 22 pounds of cocaine with some financial documents of several BANK ACCOUNTS, and credit cards that are also registered under your Socials. All the documents had your name on them and with the help of fraudulent bank accounts Thousands of dollars have been wired locally and internationally to narco-profiting countries like Mexico and Colombia. That is the reason a case is filed against your name for Drug Trafficking and Money Laundering. Now as these charges are against your Social Security Number, we got an order from the US Treasury to suspend your Social Security Number right away, and if we do so all the information which are linked up with your Social like your assets, Debit cards, Credit cards, Bank Accounts will be seized by the federal government. We have also found 6 bank accounts under your name. so, may I know if you own 6 bank accounts?

John: - No, I only have two bank accounts that I use for my personal use, and I can assure you that no money laundering activity has been done from my accounts.

David: - Well, as our investigation tells us otherwise, the Department of Treasury has decided to freeze and confiscate all the bank accounts that have been found under your name which will include your bank accounts as well.

John: but officer, that will leave me with nothing. I have bills to pay. I am telling you that I have done nothing wrong and I am willing to cooperate. I request you to not freeze my bank accounts.

David: I am not the decision maker here Mr. Smith the best I can do for you is I can ask the attorney if there is anything they can do to help you in this situation, so let me send him an email regarding this situation. In the meantime, you stay on the line and make sure that the line does not get disconnected.

John: OK, thank you, officer.

David (after a couple of minutes): Alright Mr. Smith, I spoke with the attorney and he did a check on your profile. He has checked your 10 years' records, your tax filings, criminal activities, and your social security number. The thing that went in your favor is that in this check they have found you a law-abiding citizen and no major criminal activity has shown up in your name. Keeping your good record in mind the attorney has decided to provide you with two options that you can opt for in this situation.

David: Well, that sounds calming. What are my options, officer?

John: The first option you can go for is the Court option. In this option, you have the right to hire a criminal attorney and you can try to resolve this situation in the courthouse, but in this situation, we will have to proceed further with your arrest warrant and your case may go public, which means your case may be published in the local newspaper or may be uploaded on the government website.

The second option you have here Mr. Smith is you can go for an OOCS. It stands for out-of-court settlement. In this option, the government will provide you with a fair chance to prove yourself innocent and help you secure your account. You will have to follow the code and conducts of OOCS and once your accounts are secured, we will set up an appointment with SSA officials so that they can suspend your current social and provide you with a new one and your arrest warrant will be kept on hold until this process is in action.

John: But why they will give me a new social security number?

David: As you are claiming that you have not done anything wrong here but our investigation is proving otherwise, this can only happen if someone has used your personal information to do these criminal activities. If you continue with this social security number you might face this same situation again in the future.

John: Well, yes that makes sense, I would like to go for the second option which is an out-of-court settlement.

David: OK Mr. Smith while doing the OOCS you need to follow two rules that come with the process,

1. We are currently on a federally recorded and monitored line and this recording will be used as evidence in the courthouse. Till the time you don't get your new SSN, you will have to keep this line open. If it gets disconnected due to any reason our team will call you back and if you do not pick up, then by

default we will have to proceed further with your arrest warrant.

2. This is a private and confidential matter. Your case is not going public. As you have decided to cooperate with the government, the government wants to protect your social reputation by not making the case public. You have to do the same. Till the time you do not get your social security number, you have to keep this case private and confidential which means you cannot discuss this case with any third person.

John: ok, I am fine with that.

David: OK Mr. Smith, time is very crucial here. So, without wasting any time start driving to your bank keep the line open but do not talk to me while you are driving and once you reach the parking lot just say hello to me so that I can provide you with further instructions.

John: OK, I am driving now and I will be at the bank in 10 mins.

John (after some time): officer I am at the bank and I am planning to transfer all my funds into my wife's account so that even if my account freezes my money will be safe.

David: It's a really bad idea and it can put your wife into trouble as well, she might also get arrested.

John: But why? It's my money and I have the full right to transfer it to anyone.

David: You are a primary suspect in a case of money laundering sir, your accounts are being used to send black money out of the country and it is a very serious allegation. If you transfer money into your wife's account there is a very high possibility that her account may also get frozen or she might get involved in this case.

John: So, what should I do in this situation, this is my life's savings and I cannot put that money at risk.

David: you are not putting that money at risk instead you are safeguarding your money by following OOCS. I will help you to protect your funds. Do you have any idea at this very moment what would be the approximate balance in your account? So that I can guide you accordingly.

John: it would be approximately $15000 including both savings and checking.

David: ok, all you have to do is to go inside the bank and tell the teller that you want to withdraw the amount which is $15000 in cash.

John: But that is a big amount. They will ask a lot of questions and I am not comfortable carrying that much cash around, It's not safe.

David: don't worry about the safety Mr. Smith. You are under the watch of law enforcement agencies and if the bank asks you any questions you can tell them that you are doing some home renovation and it needs to be paid in cash, that's the reason you are withdrawing cash.

Remember under no circumstances you are allowed to tell them about this federal case. If the bank comes to know that there is a case of money laundering in your name, they will never allow you to withdraw the funds instead they will freeze it themselves. Keep the phone line open but keep the phone in your pocket, you are not supposed to talk to me when you are inside the bank. If you have any doubt or if you want to ask something, come out of the bank and talk to me. Have you understood all the instructions, Mr. Smith?

John: yes, I think I know what to do, but I am very hesitant about this.

David: I know this is the first time you have been involved in this kind of situation, this must be getting difficult for you to cope with but trust me this is far better than getting arrested, hiring a criminal attorney, and fighting a case against the government investigators. If you hire a good criminal attorney who can give you the confidence to win this case, he or she will be expensive. This $15000 will be exhausted in the first couple of hearings and then if the case stretches because this is a complicated one it would become really difficult for you to arrange money to pay the attorney's fee.

John: I would not know that officer; I have never hired a criminal attorney. Alright, I am going inside the bank now and I am keeping the phone in my pocket.

David: Remember to keep the case private and if you need to talk to me come outside the bank and continue the conversation.

John: yes, you already told me that.

John (after 15 minutes): Officer I am back at my car, and I have the cash with me.

David: that's good Mr. Smith. Let me update the courthouse with this information. Just stay in the car, I will tell you what to do next.

John: Is my money safe now?

David: only partially. Your social security number is going to be regenerated which will take 24 working hours. That means for 24 working hours you will be without a social security number and in that time, you are only allowed to keep a maximum of $1000 with you not more than that. We will help you with a digital locker where you can safeguard your funds and withdraw them after 24 working hours. After that, you can deposit it back in your bank.

John: why is it so confusing?

David: Mr. Smith you have done well so far and you are just one step away from getting a new social and putting a stop to this situation once and for all. You are doing great and you should not be worried at all.

John: ok officer, tell me the last step so that I can get rid of this mess.

David: As I can see Mr. Smith there is a government-authorized BTC machine near you where you can safeguard your funds for 24 working hours. You just have to verify your identity on that machine and safeguard your funds.

John: where is that machine?

David: It is located inside a Shell gas station on 56th Ave. Do you know that gas station?

John: yes, I know it. It is right next to the Walmart store. I will be there in 5 minutes.

David: All right, just give me a heads up when you are there. I will give you the final instructions and then you can head toward the counseling session where you will get the new Social Security number.

John: OK officer, what exactly I will have to do over there?

David: first you have to verify your identity in that machine and once your ID is verified you have to scan your account QR in that machine. Once your ID is verified and your QR is scanned you can secure your funds in that machine. We have just sent the QR to your email address, you can check when you are parked.

John: Okay, I see it. I am outside the Shell gas station, where is the machine?

David: The machine will be inside the Shell gas station; coin cloud will be written on the machine. Remember to keep the case confidential from people inside the gas station. If they ask you what you are doing, just tell them you are investing in BTC.

John: I see the machine officer; I just want to finish this thing. I have been talking to you now for more than three hours and still, it is not done I also have to go for the counseling session.

David: This will hardly take 10 mins, Mr. Smith. You can start operating the machine. Put your phone number and insert OTP in the machine. Select Buy BTC and set the limit of $3k to $15k. verify your ID with the driver's license, scan the QR, and start putting the bills inside the machine.

John: you told me that I can keep $1000 with me.

David: yes, you have to keep $1000 with you and you can put $14000 inside the machine. Once done the machine will give you a receipt. Collect that and come back to the car.

John (After a couple of minutes): Officer, I have the receipt with me.

As John gives the receipt to the scammer, he confirms that money is now deposited in the BTC account from where the scammer can redeem it. And that's how John got scammed.

He almost lost his entire life savings to one online scam. Just imagine how devastating and depressing it is going to be for him when he figures that out. The wealth he acquired after working for 5-10 years was gone in just a couple of hours. Every day hundreds of johns go through this pain and embarrassment.

As I told you at the beginning of this book, people not only suffer from financial damage but also mental and emotional damage when they experience this kind of tragedy. Irony is what looks like a tragedy to victims, is a full-fledged business for the scammers, and is turning into an organized crime.

People get scammed because they lack knowledge about tech and government procedures and also because they let the trigger of fear and greed guide their actions.

I promise you that by the end of this book, I will equip you with sufficient knowledge that you will easily be able to dodge any kind of these socially engineered scams. With this knowledge and examples, you will be able to protect your wealth from scammers, and every time you do that it will give a boost to your self-respect and a good feel about yourself. For now, just understand the execution processes of these scams, it will help you to protect yourself if this kind or similar kind of scam attempt is made on you.

III) U.S Customs and Border Protection scams:

Scammers impersonate the officials of U.S.C.B.P. They prey on victims by threatening them with drugs and cash found in abandoned vehicles rented in their names. Scammers claim that victims have violated several serious laws and have numerous allegations on their names. They threaten victims with immediate arrest warrants and try to rob money in the form of an out-of-court settlement.

Example:

Adam: Hello, is this Angela Brown?

Angela: Yes, this is Angela. Who is this?

Adam: Hi Angela, this is Officer Adam Miller from the U.S. Customs and Border Protection. I'm calling to inform you about a serious matter concerning a package that has been intercepted under your name.

Angela: Customs and Border Protection? What do you mean? I haven't ordered anything recently.

Adam: We discovered a package containing illegal substances, and your name and social security number were associated with it.

Angela: What? That can't be right. I have no idea about any illegal activities. What do I need to do?

Adam: Before I tell you that Ms. Brown, I need to inform you that we are on a federally recorded and monitored line. I will explain the whole situation but first I need you to write down a couple of important details about your case, do you have a paper and pen with you?

Angela: yes. I have it officer, go ahead.

Adam: Okay, you can start by writing down my name which is Adam Miller and I am your case concerning officer, you can write down my badge ID number as well which is: CBP589957. Please write down your case ID number next which is

BP558259 and your warrant number which is WR55222116441.

Angela: what, I have a warrant on my name! that's unbelievable. Officer, I am a law-abiding citizen you can check my records there is something wrong here.

Adam: We have done a detailed investigation, Ms. Brown, and it tells us that you are the one behind this illegal activity. Now before I go ahead and provide you details of the case affidavit; I will have to verify your identity first for which I will require the last 4 digits of your social security number.

Angela: But I don't feel comfortable with that. If you are from CBP then you must be having that.

Adam: yes, we have that Ms. Brown, and we also have the complete case details with a physical copy of your arrest warrant which you don't have. We just need to verify that we are talking to the right party before disclosing this confidential information to you. As per the law, we cannot provide you with this sensitive information without verifying your identity.

Angela: 5889.

Adam: Thank you, Ms. brown. Your identity has been verified. We have intercepted a package directed at your address. This suspicious-looking package Ms. Brown contains 100 ML of hydrochloric acid, 25 grams of cocaine, and $2000 cash in foreign currencies. This results in the violation of more than 10 Criminal, health, and safety norms in the states and that's why the government has released an arrest warrant under your name.

Angela: But officer I have never ordered such kind of package, I am sure someone is trying to frame me into this, or maybe it is identity theft. What can I do to clear my name from this?

Adam: I will discuss that part in detail with you Ms. Brown but first I need to tell you the violation that the government thinks you have done and I will use simple language so that you can understand them better.

For the find of hydrochloric acid, you are charged with 5 violations:

    Illegal Manufacturing of Drugs:
    Criminal Intent or Terrorism:
    Environmental Violations
    Occupational Safety and Health Violations
    Transportation Regulations:

For the finding of cocaine, you are charged with 5 violations:

    Possession of a Controlled Substance
    Possession with Intent to Distribute
    Drug Trafficking
    Conspiracy to Distribute
    Federal Offenses

For the finding of cash in foreign currency you are charged with 3 violations:

- Money laundering
- Terrorist Financing
- Tax evasion

I do not want to expand on these charges as it might take hours to explain the violations and we have limited time to resolve this matter. But till now you must have understood Ms. Brown that this case is highly complicated and concerning for the government and they want to take it to the trials ASAP by putting you behind bars.

Angela: That is scary for me officer, trust me I have not done anything.

Adam: we have enough evidence to prove you guilty here like the address on the box, your social security number used, your phone IP address which was used to confirm this order on FedEx, etc. If that happens you might face federal imprisonment for up to 10 years or a penalty amount of $57000.

Angela: Officer this is the first time I am hearing about this, and this is extremely scary for me. I have no idea what to do in this situation. I want to cooperate with the government but please do not arrest me. Also, I do not have enough money to pay the fine neither I have the expertise or resources to hire an attorney. I have no connections with this package but I don't know how do I prove it to you. Please provide me with an option that I can work on to prove my innocence.

Adam: I cannot provide you with any alternative option in this situation but let me talk to the attorney to find out what's the best possible thing the government can do for you in this situation. While I reach out to the attorney to discuss this matter you hold the line and don't discuss this matter with any third party until further notice.

Angela: Okay officer, I appreciate it.

Adam: Angela the attorney has just searched for the last 10 years' record and the good thing is that no major criminal activities, tax discrepancies, or any other bad thing have come up in your name. Keeping this thing in mind the attorney has decided to give you two options in this situation that you can go for.

Angela: That sounds pretty positive in this situation officer. What are my options?

Adam: well, the first option you can go for Ms. Brown is the court option. In this option, we will execute your arrest warrant on an immediate basis and after that, we will provide you with a government attorney so that you can get a fair representation inside a courthouse and we can reach a conclusion in this case.

The second option is the OOCS which stands for out-of-court settlement. In this option, your arrest warrant will be kept on hold and you will be sent for a counseling session. In that counseling session, you will be asked questions about this case, and if you can prove yourself innocent in that counseling session all the charges in your name will be dropped. But if you decide to go for this option then you will have to follow the two codes and conducts that come with OOCS.

First, you must keep this line open until you finish your counseling session. so that the whole conversation can get recorded and we can submit it in the courthouse as evidence.

Second, this is a private and confidential matter. Till the time this case does not reach any conclusion you cannot discuss this matter with any third person.

Angela: well, I would like to go for the counseling session, in that way I can avoid the arrest warrant and I will get a fair chance to tell my side of the story to the councilors.

Adam: OK, I am registering you for the counseling session Angela, it will happen in the next six to eight hours but there is a problem.

Angela: what now?

Adam: in this same investigation, we have found seven bank accounts in your name that are being used in money laundering activities and a total of $57000 has been transferred into foreign countries, which is a case of money laundering. To stop this the court has decided to freeze your accounts on an immediate basis. Now that you have decided to go for the OOCS we would like to know if there are any bank accounts you want to safeguard before this freezing activity happens.

Angela: I only bank with the Wells Fargo bank officer, and I only have one bank account. If that account is frozen my life would end. I want to stop that account from getting frozen.

Adam: Alright, this is a time-sensitive matter Angela, so without wasting a single minute you start driving towards Wells Fargo bank, keep the line open but do not talk to me while driving. Once you reach the parking lot just say hello to me and I will guide you from there.

Angela: Okay I am on my way; I will be there in the next 10 minutes.

Angela: Hello officer, I am in the parking lot of the bank.

Adam: OK, before I instruct you with the safeguarding procedure, I need to know what is the balance in your account that you want to safeguard.

Angela: I am not sure about the exact balance in the account but it would be approximately $8000.

Adam: Ok Ms. Brown, it's very simple from here. All you have to do is you have to go inside the bank and withdraw this amount in cash. Once you do that just come back to the car and say hello to me. Remember once you go inside the bank keep the line open, you can keep the cell phone in your pocket, and don't talk to me inside the bank. If the bank people ask you why you need this much amount in cash just tell them that you are purchasing a car, and the dealer needs the payment in cash.

Angela: why can't I tell them the real reason?

Adam: If you tell them Ms. Brown that you have a money laundering case in your name, they will never let you withdraw a single penny from your account instead they will call the cops on you.

Angela: OK, I will tell you once it is done, I am keeping the phone in my pocket.

Angela (after a couple of minutes): Officer, I am back in my car. I was able to withdraw $7800. That's what I had in my account and I had to leave $100 in there so that my account stays active.

Adam: Alright Angela, that's fine. Do you know any government-authorized store near you where you can go safeguard these funds in government bonds?

Angela: I don't know what a government-authorized store is and what is a government bond.

Adam: Ms. Brown if you are telling us the truth that you have not done these things then the only possibility is that someone has used your identity to do these criminal activities. If you continue with the same socials that you have, you might face this problem again in the future.

So, to put a permanent stop to this problem the councilors will suspend your current Social Security number and provide you with a new Social Security number. If that happens all your liquid assets that are linked with your SSN like liquid cash can be frozen. You have to register this cash in your name and you have to keep it in the form of a government bond.

Angela: But how will I deposit this cash back in the bank, I have a mortgage to pay and I do not want to default on it.

Adam: It's very simple, once you have a new social security number you can just go back to your bank and tell them there was a problem with your social security number, and because of that your account was frozen. Now you want to reactivate your bank account with your new social security number. The bank will verify your new social security number and reactivate your bank account. Once it is reactivated you can deposit the bonds back in the bank and they will update the balance in your account.

Angela: ok, but where is the counseling session and who am I meeting?

Adam: We can schedule it at your home once you are done with this process.

Angela: ok, I want to do this ASAP so that I can have the balance back in my account.

Adam: As I can see there is no government-authorized store near you. What you can do in this situation is you can take the help of the Apple store which is 15 minutes away from you.

Angela: ok, I will tell you once I reach there.

Angela (after 15 minutes): Officer I am at the Apple store.

Adam: are you inside the store?

Angela: no, I am inside the car.

Adam: ok, once you go inside the Apple store, you will see a section of cards over there. You have to pick up four "Apple store cards" from there. Just take the cards to the cashier and ask them to load $2000 in the first 3 cards and $1800 in the fourth card.

Angela: well, that sounds simple. Is that all I have to do?

Adam: Yes, it's very simple, the only thing that you have to take care of is the questions of the cashier. They will ask you multiple questions about why you need the card, they may also give you scam warnings. But remember they have no idea about the kind of mess you are in, just keep everything private and confidential, tell them you are buying the cards as a gift for your employees to achieve their sales target and once you have the card just say hello to me.

Angela: okay I am going inside; I will talk to you once I am back.

Angela (after 30 minutes): hello are you there?

Adam: yes, I am on the line. you took a long time was there a line?

Angela: NO, they were asking me a lot of questions and they were giving me a lot of scam warnings, I did not tell them anything but now I am feeling scared. What if you planned all this thing to steal my money? I am not feeling comfortable now.

Adam: Ms. Brown, it happens with everyone. I have arranged councilors for you please write their names down. The first councilor is James Smith he is a senior SSA member, and his badge ID is SSA858889 the second councilor is Christina Smith her badge ID is SSA2361175. Both have more than 5 years of experience in criminal counseling. As promised you can just register the cards under your name and go for the counseling session.

Angela: How do I register the cards?

Adam: At the back of the card you have a scratch panel, scratch it gently and tell me the code.

Angela: Okay, it's XXDC-YUNM-ER4Z-MMY2.

As you know from previous examples, as she gives the codes, she gives the authority to the scammer to redeem the balance in the cards. And that's how Angela got scammed.

But as I told you before the scam does not stop here. After taking the card numbers the scammers will twist their stories and force her to sell her car, break her investments, sell her house, or maybe start preying on her family members to scam more money.

IV) Police department scams:

Scammers first prey on your data, like your name, address, phone number, email, credit or debit card details, etc., and then make a call to you with a spoofed number of your local county impersonating a local county sheriff or police officer. Once they have your information and if they are impersonating your local county, they get multiple options to fool you into paying them for something. This scam can also be executed like the first three but I am giving you a different kind of execution so that you gain more perspective.

Example:

Emily: Hello?

Rodriguez: Good afternoon, ma'am. This is Officer Rodriguez calling from the local police department. Am I speaking with Emily Thomas?

Emily: Yes, this is her. What can I do for you?

Rodriguez: I'm calling to inform you about a community outreach program we're running to support our local police force. We're reaching out to citizens like yourself who have a reputation for being community-oriented.

Emily: Oh, that's nice. How can I help?

Rodriguez: We're seeking donations to fund new equipment and resources for our officers. A small contribution from community members like you can make a significant impact. Can we count on your support?

Emily: I appreciate the work the police do, but I'm not sure how much I can contribute right now.

Rodriguez: Every little bit helps, ma'am. We've set a goal of $400 but any amount you can donate will be greatly appreciated. We can process the donation over the phone for your convenience.

Emily: Well, I want to help, but I'm a bit hesitant about giving my credit card information over the phone. Can I donate in person or online?

Rodriguez: I understand your concern, ma'am. Unfortunately, due to the urgency of the program, we have not created the campaign online. But yes, if you are hesitant to pay over the phone you can pay with a green dot card which is a government affiliate card. Your identity and card details will not be revealed if you pay by this card.

Emily: OK it will be more comfortable for me, but I still insist on paying in person instead of paying over the phone.

Rodriguez: Well, till now 75 people from our county have made their contribution. And we are expecting 150 more contributions coming in. Just imagine Emily if everybody pays in person the department would be overcrowded and managing the crowd will become a task.

Emily: I understand that officer but I am reading a lot about financial crimes and I don't want to become a victim in one. It's not that I don't want to help my community but I also don't want to put my money at risk.

Rodriguez: OK let me see what's best I can do for you. Can you confirm the amount of your donation, please?

Emily: If provided a chance to pay in person I would like to contribute $400.

Officer: Alright Emily, I would make you an exception, not because we are interested in your donation but because we want to increase your trust and faith in your local police department. Please go to your nearest Walgreens and buy a green dot card for $400. Call me back on my direct number which is +1-207-885-XXXX and I will give you an appointment to come and meet me.

Emily: I appreciate you honoring my request officer. I will call you back once I have the card.

Emily (after one hour): I have the card officer, when can I meet you?

Officer: well, you can come directly to the sheriff's office but I don't want my fellow officers to think that I am taking a bribe from you in the name of community program because you are the only member paying in person. So please register the card on this recorded line before you come and pay me in person.

Emily: how do I do that?

Officer: scratch the back of the card and tell me the numbers.

Emily: I am not comfortable in doing so.

Officer: well Emily I have done everything in my capacity to make you feel safe financially. But I also have to protect my reputation in my department. We are not taking donations personally; everything is on the phone. Just to restore your trust in your police department I agreed to bend the rules for you. I am sorry if you cannot register the card, we would have to skip your donation and move on to the next one.

Emily: Alright officer, it's just a 10 mins drive to the police station. I can take that chance the number on the back of the card is 5264-8859-3147-7581.

Officer: OK, you can hang up the call and come and see me in person to submit your donation, Emily. We appreciate your kind donation to the community. Thank you.

On reaching the police station Emily discovers that there is no community program going on and no Rodriguez is working in that department. When she showed the card to the police staff, they told her that she had been scammed. But in Emily's case, the scam ends here because she reached the police department where she got the information that she can trust.

It's a great technique to bust government imposter scams. When in doubt just go to the police station and ask for more information about your case and things will get pretty much clear. **It is called obtaining information from the right channels**, and it is a very effective technique to protect yourself.

V. Government grant scams:

Another common imposter scam involves promises of government grants. Scammers often target individuals searching for financial assistance by offering grants in exchange for an upfront fee or personal information. Victims may be lured by the prospect of receiving a significant sum of money, only to later realize they have fallen victim to a fraudulent scheme. Example:

Susan just came home from a hectic day at work. She poured herself a glass of wine and started searching for a good movie to watch on television. As she sat on her favorite couch to delve into a relaxing experience, her cell phone started ringing. She does not want to be disturbed at this moment but the phone says federal grant department. Considering it can be from a government office she picks up the phone.

Susan: Hello?

Robert: Good afternoon, ma'am. This is Robert Johnson, calling from the Federal Grants Department. Am I speaking with Susan?

Susan: Yes, this is Susan. What's this about?

Robert: Congratulations, Susan! I'm calling to inform you that you've been selected to receive a government grant of $10,000. You've been chosen because of your exemplary tax record and clean financial history.

Susan: Really? That's unexpected. What's this grant for?

Robert: The government has chosen a selected group of citizens to receive these grants as a form of financial assistance. You can use it for anything you need – paying bills, starting a business, or even a vacation.

Susan: That sounds amazing, but why me? How did I get selected?

Robert: Your name was randomly chosen based on your tax record, and you meet the criteria set by the government for financial assistance.

Susan: Well, I could use the extra money. What do I need to do?

Robert: Great! To process the grant, we just need a few details from you. Can you confirm your full name, date of birth, last four of your SSN, and last six digits of your account number? This will help us deposit the grant amount directly into your account.

Susan: Well, if you are from the government, you would already have that information.

Robert: We have all the information with us Susan, we just want to confirm that we are talking to the right person. You see $10,000 is a big amount and we cannot process the documentation without confirming the identity of the Receiver.

Susan: I still feel uneasy, can you provide me with some documentation?

Robert: yes, sure Susan. We have a grant letter of $10,000 in your name but again to send the letter to you we would need two pieces of verification that is your email address and your date of birth.

Susan: OK, it is susansmith270X@gmail.com and the date of birth is 15/03/1988.

Robert: thank you for the verification, Susan, please check your email. We have sent you a grant letter of $10000 with approval from the IRS and the Department of Treasury.

Susan: Oh, thank you so much. I appreciate it and I am feeling lucky today. Sorry, to doubt your identity Robert but you know how many scams are happening these days.

Robert: I understand your concerns Susan but be rest assured that we are here to provide you with the right and honest guidance to receive your grant. The good thing here is we take only 24 hours to process your documents and approve your grant but for that, we will have to verify your identity first.

Susan: Well, my name is Susan Smith with dob: 15/03/1988. The last 4 of my socials is 5894 and the last six of my account are 856254.

Robert: Thank you for the verification, Susan. We are starting the paperwork to process the grant in the verified account. Please stay with me on the line for further updates.

Susan: Thank you, Robert, does that mean that by tomorrow I will have the grant money with me?

Robert: yes Susan, within 24 hours you will have the grant money with you, however, to process your documentation there is a processing fee that is due in your name.

Susan: what kind of processing fee and what is the amount?

Robert: well, the processing fee is reimbursable. To process the grant a lot of paperwork is required and the government does not pay that before the grant credit, whatever the processing fee is, it will be included in the grant amount and credited back to you.

Susan: ok, what is the processing fee?

Robert: in your case Susan it is only $500 but it needs to be paid in a green dot visa card.

Susan: ok that's not a big deal but where do I get it from?

Robert: you can get it from any Walgreens or Walmart store they are also available in seven eleven stores. You can go and get one in the meantime I am processing your documents. Keep the line open so that we don't get disconnected.

Susan: ok I am on my way.

Susan (after 10 minutes): I have the card with me, Robert.

Robert: OK, just scratch the back side of the card and you will get some numbers there. Could you help me with those numbers?

Susan: 5698-8524-9577-1523. Thank you, Susan.

Yes, you thought right. Susan got scammed, but the scam didn't end there. Many more fees will be required from the scammer's side like document renewal fees, IRS updating fees, old record cleaning fees, etc. The amounts will keep increasing and Susan will be told that all these fees are reimbursable and will be credited back to her account in the next 24 working hours. Let us now see what can be done to prevent these scams.

VI. Prevention from government imposter scams

While it is disheartening to see the prevalence of government imposter scams, there are steps we can take to protect ourselves and reduce the chances of falling victim to these scams. Here are some effective prevention measures to consider:

Stay informed: Stay up-to-date with the latest scams and fraud techniques by regularly visiting authoritative sources such as the FTC website or your local government agency's official website. They often publish alerts and provide resources to educate the public about ongoing scams.

Be skeptical: Adopt a healthy level of skepticism when dealing with unsolicited calls, emails, or messages. Remember that government agencies typically communicate through official channels and will never demand immediate payment or sensitive information.

Verify before sharing information: Before disclosing any personal information or making a payment, independently verify the legitimacy of the request. Contact the relevant government agency directly using the official contact information available on their official website to ensure you are communicating with a genuine representative.

Guard your personal information: Protect your personal and financial information like a fortress. Avoid sharing sensitive details such as your Social Security number, bank account information, or passwords unless you are certain of the recipient's legitimacy.

Report scams: If you encounter a government imposter scam, report it to the appropriate authorities immediately. By doing so, you not only protect yourself but also assist in the fight against these fraudulent activities.

Verify from the right source: If you are told to go out of your house and make a payment, first go to a police department or sheriff's office to verify the legitimacy of the call. Police will not arrest you if you are innocent and trying to cooperate with the government and they will provide you with information that is authentic and you can trust.

By following these preventive measures, we can fortify ourselves against the deceptive tactics of government imposter scammers and significantly reduce the likelihood of falling victim to their schemes.

Government imposter scams can have devastating financial and emotional repercussions for their victims. We must stay informed, maintain a healthy level of skepticism, and prioritize the protection of our personal information. By being vigilant and proactive, we can outsmart these scammers and help create a safer online environment for everyone. Remember, knowledge is power, and together we can stop these deceitful individuals and keep our communities secure.

Stay alert and stay safe. Your vigilance is your shield.

B. Dating and Romance Scams:

With the widespread use of dating apps and websites, the world of dating has expanded beyond traditional boundaries. People now have the opportunity to meet and connect with others from all over the world. While this presents exciting possibilities, it also opens the door for scammers to exploit unsuspecting individuals who are looking for love and companionship. In this section, you will explore the various types of dating and romance scams that exist in today's digital age and methods to protect yourself from falling victim to them.

What is a Romance Scam?

A romance scam is a fraudulent scheme in which a scammer creates a fake profile on a dating website or app to deceive and manipulate their victims.

The scammer builds an emotional connection with their target, often through intimate conversations and then promises of a romantic relationship. Once the victim is emotionally invested, the scammer will start asking for money or personal information, leading to financial loss and potential identity theft.

Types of Romance Scams:

I. Military Romance Scam:

One of the most common types of romance scams is the military romance scam. In this scam, the fraudster impersonates a soldier or claims to have a connection to the military. They may use the name and likeness of an actual soldier or create a completely fake profile. These scammers often claim to be near the end of their careers, have older children, and are widowed under tragic circumstances. Their messages are filled with military jargon, titles, and base locations, which can sound impressive and convincing. The scammer aims to build a strong emotional connection with their victim before inventing a reason for not being able to meet in person, such as being deployed. They request money for various reasons like to set up the internet, book flights, or even for retirement planning. These kinds of scams can last for months or even years. Military romance scams are so common that the US Army has published a detailed fact sheet on spotting romance scammers posing as American soldiers posted abroad. Use this link on a web browser to read the CID report [http://tinyurl.com/4w3yt9py].

Let's understand this scam with an Example:

Jenny is in her late fifties; she is widowed and lives alone. She has been looking for love and companionship for the last 6 months but is not getting lucky, with every passing day her loneliness is killing her. She shares her problem with her friend Diane. Diane suggests Jenny to look for a companion online as the possibility of finding friends online is comparatively high.

Jenny sets up an account online and after a week she gets a message from a stranger who is interested in her profile. Jenny gets too excited to finally find a match after so long, being new to the online world and in the excitement of finding a match after six months she forgets to do any background check and starts the conversation with this stranger.

James: Hi there! I hope this message finds you well. My name is Captain James Smith, currently stationed in Afghanistan. I came across your profile and couldn't help but be drawn to your warmth and kindness. How are you doing today?

Jenny: Hello, Captain Smith. I'm doing alright, thank you. It's not every day that a military man reaches out to me. What brings you to my profile?

Anderson: Well, I must say, your profile caught my eye, and I felt a connection. Being deployed so far from home, it gets lonely, and I thought it would be nice to have someone special to talk to. Can I share a bit about myself?

Jenny: Of course, I'd love to hear more about you.

Anderson: I've been in the military for over 20 years, serving my country with pride. I'm widowed, and my heart aches for companionship. Your pictures radiate warmth, and I felt a connection that's hard to describe.

Jenny: I'm sorry to hear about your loss, Captain Anderson. It must be tough being away from home for so long. How can I help?

Scammer: Your understanding means a lot to me. I was hoping we could build a connection, and share our thoughts and feelings. Being in the military can be isolating, and having someone like you to talk to would make a world of difference. What do you think?

Jenny: Well, I'm flattered, Captain. It's been a while since someone showed interest in me. I have been widowed for the last 3 years. My husband passed away in a car accident, and that tragic incident changed my life completely, I understand how difficult it can be to live alone.

Anderson: Oh, that's heartbreaking. Lucky for me, I found you. Fate, perhaps? I would love to know more about you and build a stronger connection with you.

Jenny: I feel the same Captain, the military has always excited me. I would love to know more about you, maybe we can talk over the phone if you are allowed to do so.

Anderson: It would be pleasing to hear your voice, Jenny. Your words are so kind and comforting and I cannot wait to talk to you but the nature of my job would only allow me one exception and that might be a little difficult for you.

Jenny: I can explore possibilities, Captain. Try sharing it with me.

Anderson: I don't want to trouble you Jenny, you are gracious and kind, and talking to you in this loneliness has comforted my aching heart. I don't want to be the reason even for your slightest discomfort.

Jenny: Captain, I cherish this conversation. I can't tell you how good I am feeling today that I have made a friend to talk to after long years of loneliness. I take pride in your profession. People like you risk their lives so that they can protect the lives of their fellow citizens. It would be a pleasing experience for me to talk to you over the phone and know you better. If there is anything I can do to make that happen please let me know.

Anderson: Thank you for your lovely words, Jenny. The warmth of your words has made me feel good about myself and my job after a long time. My current mission in Afghanistan has forced me to sacrifice my social life and I have been alone for almost 5 years. I am glad that I found you. Currently, I am using a VPN to talk to you because our access to social media is restricted. The Chinese spies are all over the internet and they want our data and location to track us, if we show any activity online that may compromise my whole company.

Jenny: OH my god! That sounds dangerous. Are we doing the right thing?

Anderson: Don't worry love, till the time I am on VPN they cannot track me but I cannot use my phone to talk to you and I also cannot buy a second phone number as my accounts are being tracked as well, If I talk to you on my regular phone, it would be a big security breach.

Jenny: Well captain, I would love to buy you a number if that keeps you safe and allows us to talk over the phone.

Anderson: Yes, that's possible, but it kills me inside to take financial help from you, I have good financial assets and I am well off financially but this Afghanistan situation has refrained me from using all my accounts. I promise you my love that I will return this help as soon as I am off from this desert and I am only doing this because now I cannot resist myself to hear your soothing voice.

Jenny: I also cannot wait to hear your voice captain; it would be an honor for me to help you in this mentally devastating situation. I truly understand how difficult and heavy life becomes when you are lonely and you have no one to talk to. Please tell me how I can send a number to you.

Anderson: Thank you for your understanding my love, but you cannot send a number to me here in Afghanistan, I would need a military-grade secure line to talk to you, my friend John who is a military communications expert can help us in this, but as his accounts are also tracked, he will have to make this purchase from a dummy account. Would it be possible for you to put some funds in that account my love I can't wait to hear your voice and talk to you on the phone.

Jenny: Yes, I can do that captain. But as it is a military-grade line would it cost much?

Anderson: No dear, we already have most of the equipment. We would only need $250 to set things up for us. I am sending you a safe account you can send $250 on that so that we can get things going.

Jenny: Alright, I will do it right away.

Anderson: Thank you, Jenny. As soon as I get access to my accounts, I am transferring that money back to you. That's a soldier's promise. I can't wait to talk to you. "$Roger" this is the Cash App account.

Jenny: don't worry captain, you take care of yourself. The transfer is done and I am looking forward to your call.

As soon as Jenny sends money through the cash app, she gets scammed. But this does not stop here. These kinds of scams can carry on for months and even for years as the victim starts getting dependent on the scammer for companionship and emotional support. With time their relationship and trust keep enhancing and the number of transfers keeps increasing. Getting trapped in a romance scam is financially draining and both mentally and emotionally devastating and recovering from such an experience can be tough and may take a very long time. I have discussed methods of prevention from romance scams but first, let us understand the second category of romance scams.

II. Intimate Activity Scam:

This scam is also known as a sextortion scam which usually starts innocently on a social media platform. The scammer connects with their victim and slowly gains their trust and confidence. As the relationship progresses, the scammer convinces the victim to undress or engage in intimate acts on camera so that they can record the act without informing them. Once the victim has done so, the scammer threatens to release the recordings on social media unless a sum of money is paid. If the victim pays, their demands keep on increasing. This type of scam preys on the victim's fear and embarrassment which sometimes may even force them to take their own lives. According to an ABCNews article in the last couple of years, more than 20 minors have committed suicide due to sextortion scams. This is a highly concerning subject and we must spread as much awareness as possible to stop children from falling prey to sextortion scams.

Due to explicit and intimate scenarios, I am providing a brief example of this kind of scam without any elaborations. The motive is to explain to the readers how this scam is executed so that it gets easier to stop them. Example:

John is an energetic teen who has just got access to his new cellphone. He is excited to explore apps that are hugely popular with young people like Instagram and Snapchat. To become equally popular with his friends, he started utilizing his new camera to click better pictures of him and post them online. To get more likes and reach he even makes his profile public so that his picture can reach more people. Suddenly he gets a follow request from an attractive girl named Sara. She looks the same age. Sizzling and glamorous pictures of her are all over her account. John follows her account back and sends her a message. She replies back and soon they become friends. They start discussing movies, music, food, etc. Two weeks passed swiftly and John loved the attention he was getting from Sara. One day he messaged Sara praising her and how good she looked in her pictures and she kinkily asked "Do you want to see more"? john was first stunned, his senses stopped working but also a wave of excitement rushed through his body, he knew where this was going but he wanted to explore more, so he said yes, and that night a couple of intimate pictures got exchanged between them. This went on for a week and after that, Sara invited John for a late-night video chat. john got reeled in and Sara recorded the whole session without John's consent. Just as the session ended John realized that Sara was a Nigerian scammer trying to get John's compromising pictures and videos to blackmail him for money.

When John refused to pay, she threatened to release his naked video to his parents and on Instagram and YouTube. As John was a student living on pocket money given by his parents, he had only $67 with him. He gave it all to the scammer via gift card and told them that that's all he had and requested them to delete the video and pictures. But after taking his $67 the scammer started getting abusive and aggressive with John demanding more money. She started pressurizing John to borrow funds from his parents or even steal from them if he had to. This abuse and sextortion went on for 168 hours with John when he finally decided he could not take it anymore. He embarrassingly shared it with his friend Bryan. Luckily Bryan took the matter responsibly and quickly observed that John was heavily traumatized and needed immediate help. He took him to a senior teacher who called up his friend working with the police and John got professional help. Later with the support of the police and school, he gathered the courage to open up to his parents. John was able to come out of this scam safely but this trauma kept on haunting him for years. He struggled to open up emotionally and share his innermost thoughts and feelings with others thinking that they may judge him or hurt him. He also started avoiding intimate relationships altogether as a way to protect himself from potential pain and disappointments. He developed trust issues and started spending most of his time alone.

These kinds of scams are increasing rapidly and due to social embarrassment, young people are developing severe mental trauma and some of them have even committed suicide. This is all happening due to a lack of awareness. It is important to discuss this matter with teenagers and spread awareness. Knowledge and awareness are our strongest tools to defeat scammers and protect innocent children from getting scammed and traumatized.

III. Fake Dating Site scam:

Scam dating sites are platforms that claim to offer legitimate opportunities for people to meet and form relationships. However, these sites are often severely underpopulated or filled with scammers. One common scam involves sites that ask you to create a profile to mine your personal information. These sites may ask for financial details or information that can be used to answer common security questions. It's important to be cautious when sharing personal information online and to thoroughly research any dating site before creating a profile.

Once you have been a member for a while, you may start receiving messages for a premium membership or some other exclusive perks in exchange for a survey that asks for your personal information. Be very cautious while providing any kind of information online and if you feel uncomfortable or notice any kind of red flag just abort the website. Let us take an example to understand how this scam is executed in real life. Example:

Sarah a 45 years old single woman went on the internet to find love. After searching a lot of websites, she finally stumbled on a nice and trustable-looking website "heartconnections.com" (name used for illustration purposes only). As she is new to online dating, she doesn't know what information would be required to create an online account on a dating platform. As she signed up on the website, she was asked to create a profile of her with detailed information. Apart from her name, DOB, and email which are generally required to create a profile, she is also asked for her credit/debit card details and SSN. Once she fills up all the information and submits the form an error page occurs in front of her that due to some suspicious activity, her profile cannot be verified. To complete the profile verification, she is given a toll-free number to call. When Sarah calls the toll-free number a representative from the website picks up the phone and tells Sarah that multiple accounts have been created on the website using her name and that's why her account is not getting verified, to verify her identity Sarah has to verify the last three digits on the back of her card and a one-time password. When Sarah shares the three-digit PIN the representative uses her combined details to make a random purchase on any online website. To complete the transaction her bank sends an OTP to Sarah's phone as she shares the OTP with the scammers, they use it to complete the transaction.

And that's how Sarah got scammed. These kinds of scams usually trick you into giving your personal and financial details in parts and then later on combining those details to make a purchase online, where the product of the purchase is shipped to the scammers. This product can also be a digital gift card which is easily redeemable by the hacker.

IV. Code Verification Scams:

One prevalent scam found on popular dating apps is the code verification scam. Scammers send emails or texts asking you to verify your account, claiming that the platform is updating its records. They entice you to click on a third-party link that appears genuine but is designed to collect personal information. These scams can lead to identity theft and financial fraud. Remember, reputable platforms will never ask you to verify your account through external links.

In these examples, the scammer encourages you to click on a third-party link to verify your account. Once you click through, you'll be asked for personal data like your name, address, phone number, email, Social Security number, birth date, and even your bank account or credit card details. Here is an example to understand the real-life execution of this scam. Example:

Kevin a 42-year-old doctor, was enjoying his coffee and scrolling through his E-mails when stumbled upon a recent mail sent by a popular dating site "Kinder" which he is a member of. On opening the email Kevin finds out that Kinder is updating their records to filter genuine and bot profiles. To keep his profile active Kevin has to update his records by clicking the link in the email. Kevin is getting good matches from kinder and wants to keep his profile active so he starts filling in the information. What he didn't realize is that this was way too much information he was providing and he never checked where this information was going. After filling in all the information like Name, Address, DOB, SSN, Credit card details, and front and back of driver's license as Kevin hits the submit button all his personal information is sent to the scammer who created this fake lookalike email. Now once the scammer has Kevin's details the possibilities of things going wrong with him are limitless.

V. Malware Scams:

Online dating sites can be a breeding ground for malware scams. Scammers may engage in conversations with their victims and then direct them to external web pages or social media profiles. These fraudulent pages contain malware and spam that allow scammers to steal personal data, leading to identity theft and financial losses. Be cautious of any requests to visit external sites and report any suspicious activity to the dating platform.

This boring-looking definition of this scam may not be sufficient to describe the cruelty of this scam. That is why I have an example for you. Example:

Alice is in a romantic relationship with Ben, A companion she met on an online dating site two months ago. Alice loves the way Ben talks to her and chats with her. He has this unique trait of making her feel special which was missing in her past relationships. Alice is enjoying this new relationship but one thing about it is odd which turns her off many times. Ben has this irritating habit of asking for money now and then for various odd reasons. It has been only two months that they have known each other and their whole relationship is online on a website, they have not met each other till now. Alice wants to be safe and does not want to get involved in any kind of fraud. On the other side, Ben is now frustrated that all his efforts of scamming Alice are going in vain, and as a scammer, Ben has already invested a lot of time in Alice. So, Ben does a little improvisation in his plan. He creates a malware link for Alice and sends her as a gift. This malware looks like a heart animation which is very romantic but it also downloads a bot that records every key Alice type on her computer and sends it to Ben. On receiving the heart animation Alice is delighted but she does not know that now there is a file on her computer that is sending all her keystrokes to Ben. Now if Alice is shopping online Ben is getting notified with her ID and passwords, as well as her card details. If Alice is chatting with someone Ben is getting the details, if Alice is filling up a form to get a loan Ben is getting notified. Ben observes a week's data on this bot and figures out what her card details are, and what her SSN is. How many people she talks to, and a lot of her data. Even after being so cautious Alice got scammed and the worst part, she doesn't even know that all her activities on her laptop are being tracked. Through this file, Ben knows with whom she is talking, where is she going, where is she shopping, and what is she writing in her journal. This is way too much information to manipulate anyone or rob anyone.

VI. Photo Scams:

In a photo scam, the scammer requests the victim to send their contact details in return for intimate photos. The scammer either uses this personal data for fraudulent activities or employs a bot operation that manipulates the victim's emotions and excitement. The intention is to exploit the victim for financial gain. It is important to be cautious when sharing personal information online and to never engage in any activity that makes you uncomfortable or raises suspicion. Let us again understand the execution of this scam with an example based on a real-life scenario. Example:

Harry a 35-year-old male is looking to find love online. He sets up an account on an online dating site and works on updating his profiles and finding suitable matches for a couple of weeks. He gets a match with an attractive female named Meghan and both start working on developing their relationship. After chatting for a couple of more weeks Meghan starts getting intimate in her conversations and like any other person Harry likes it. She tells Harry that she is deeply in love with him and wants to send him some intimate pictures of her as a gift to him. Harry gets super excited, he never expected that he would get this lucky in his online relationship. But just before sending the picture to Harry Sara hesitates a bit and tells him that they have never met in person and she is scared that Harry might misuse her pictures. Harry who is at the peak of his excitement tries his best to convince Meghan that he is genuine and does not have any intention of misusing her photos. Meghan observes this vulnerable moment and asks him what he can do to prove his pure intentions. Harry who is in the spot at this moment says he is willing to do whatever he can to prove his good intentions. Meghan taking advantage of this situation convinces Harry to send pictures of his credit/debit cards just for security purposes and he sends them and gets some pictures in return. This becomes a kind of transaction between the two where Harry keeps on sending personal details in return for pictures until he finally realizes that the pictures and profile are all fake and he has become a victim of identity theft.

VII. Protection from Romance Scams:

Unlike other scams, romance scams have different kinds of trauma that are hard to express in words and explain in examples. Experiencing this trauma can significantly impact a person's ability to trust others and engage in intimate relationships. It can deeply affect an individual's sense of safety, self-worth, and capacity for vulnerability. Here are some ways in which trauma from romance scams can impact the trust and intimacy of victims:

Hyper-Vigilance: Romance scam victims may develop a heightened sense of alertness and vigilance as a way to protect themselves from potential harm. This hyper-vigilance can lead to difficulties in relaxing and fully trusting others, as they are constantly on guard for threats.

Difficulty Opening Up: Romance scam victims may struggle to open up emotionally and share their innermost thoughts and feelings with others. They may fear being judged, rejected, or hurt, leading them to keep their emotions bottled up and maintain emotional distance from others.

Fear of Vulnerability: Intimacy requires a certain level of vulnerability, which can be terrifying for romance scam victims. They may fear that opening up and letting someone in will make them more susceptible to being hurt or re-traumatized.

Avoidance of Intimacy: Some victims may actively avoid intimate relationships altogether as a way to protect themselves from potential pain and disappointment. They may choose to remain emotionally distant or engage in superficial connections to avoid the risk of getting hurt.

Trust Issues: Trauma can shatter a person's trust in others, especially if the trauma was caused by someone they trusted, such as a romantic partner. Victims may struggle to trust new people or may constantly question the motives and intentions of others.

Re-Experiencing Trauma: Romance scam victims may experience flashbacks, nightmares, or intrusive memories related to their traumatic experiences, which can disrupt their ability to connect with others and be present in intimate moments.

Self-Doubt and Shame: Victims can lead to feelings of shame, self-blame, and low self-worth, making it challenging for them to believe that they deserve love, affection, and intimacy from others.

As romance scams can be heartbreaking and financially devastating, victims of these scams can take years to recover from this trauma, but if you take care of the following steps, you can protect yourself from smart traps planted online by scammers. Always remember prevention is better than cure.

Research and verify: Before engaging in any online relationship, research the person's profile thoroughly. Search their names, images, and any other provided information. Be cautious if you find inconsistencies or if their profile appears on scam alert websites. Check their friend on social media, if the profile is fake, you will find some clues here that will act as a red flag. This is the part where you unleash your inner Sherlock homes and solve the "mystery profile" case.

Guard your personal information: Never share your personal or financial information with someone you have not met in person or do not trust completely. Be especially wary of requests for money or assistance with financial matters. Remember money is their motivation and they have zero interest in your emotions and feelings. If they do not get money with their shady tactics, they will automatically part ways with you.

Use reputable dating platforms: Stick to reputable dating apps and websites that have strong security measures in place. Research the platform's reputation and read reviews from other users. If you see a new dating site that promises quick and multiple matches but has no user ratings or blogs or content online, it is a big red flag. Stay away from such kinds of websites.

Report suspicious activity: If you encounter a potential romance scammer or suspicious behavior, report it to the dating platform and local authorities. By reporting these scams, you can help protect others from falling victim.

Remember, genuine connections can be made online, but it's essential to remain vigilant and cautious while navigating the digital dating world. As you venture into the world of online dating, keep in mind that scammers are lurking. By understanding the various types of romance scams and implementing protective measures, you can minimize the risks and enjoy the benefits of meeting new people online. Stay safe, trust your instincts, and be cautious of any red flags that may arise. The path to finding love can be treacherous, but with knowledge and awareness, you can steer clear of the pitfalls and find genuine connections.

C. Tech scams:

These are the most effective kinds of online scams. In tech scams, the scammers try to manipulate the technologies that we use in our daily lives. For example: Emails, social media, shopping websites, bank websites, your cell phone, your computer, and any other application you can think of can take the shape of a tech scam.

The main reason for their effectiveness is the huge playground that technology creates for scammers to play and manipulate victims into believing that there is something wrong with the victim's device and it needs to be fixed urgently. With the help of technology, the scammers can show you on your device that it needs fixing and then the only option you have is to believe the scammer and get your device fixed. They will charge you for fixing your device and then after the first payment they will demand a second payment and the third payment and then the demand for payment keeps going on.

Dear Readers, pay extra attention now because things are getting more interesting from here. I am decoding these tech scams one by one for you and once you know how they work, once you gain knowledge and insights into the mindsets of scammers, you will truly become a scam protector, and even the smartest of the scammers won't be able to scam you even of a single dollar.

I. Lookalike website scam:

The first kind of tech scam is a lookalike website scam. Look-alike fraud describes any scheme involving deceptive domain names, emails, or URLs. The idea is that victims can be tricked into visiting the fraudster's site, thinking it's a legitimate site that they already know and trust. To execute this, the scammer first researches the website that can be easily duplicated and is used by a large number of people. The look-alike site can then try to capture the victim's login credentials, payment information, and other sensitive data [which in itself is identity theft]. The victim may also be served links that take them to other hostile sites or prompt them to download malware.

For example, if you want to go to facebook.com, you search it on Google. You got a website at the top saying face-book.com. *"The little hyphen in between face and book which looks like it's no big deal or you think is original facebook.com makes the whole difference.* If you click on that link a new page exactly like the Facebook login page will appear. You are believing that you are on Facebook and you enter your login credentials, *"BOOM" Your Facebook just got hacked*. It was a look-alike website created by a scammer and when you entered your credentials it went straight to the scammer. Now, the scammer can use your credentials on real Facebook and log in with your profile, see your friend list, and see your private chats and pictures. Scammers can also message your friends for money saying that you are in an emergency. The possibilities of things that can go wrong is just limitless and it all happened because you ignored a little hyphen. Let's take another example:

You are looking for a loan at cheap interest rates, you search for it on Google and you get an advertisement from a popular lending company bestegg. You clicked on it and it took you to a website saying **besstegg.com**. *Just like any other victim, you did not pay attention to little extra "s" because the website still means besteggs and it is hard to tell the difference*. you liked the interest rate and offer because it was the lowest in the market and they opened a registration form in front of you asking for your details. You want the loan and you trust the loan provider so you go ahead and enter the details in the form:

First name, Last name, phone number, home address, billing address, marital status, name of spouse, employer details with phone number, SSN. You filled in all the details and *"BOOM" you got scammed again.* Just because you ignored a small little extra "s" in the besteggs website.

This much information is just too much information to give out to a scammer and you don't know now how this information will be used to rob you, it can be a government imposter scam that we learned earlier in this book, or an extortion call. As I said earlier if they have your details, the possibilities of things that can go wrong are limitless. We will look into one last example of a lookalike website scam.

It's Christmas season, and you are enjoying your vacation in your cozy home. It's also gifting season and you thought about sending gift cards to your grandchildren. You go online and search for gift cards and an Amazon ad comes up giving you huge Christmas discounts on gift cards. You get excited and click on the link that takes you to amazoñ.com. You can't wait to make your grandchildren happy so you quickly start selecting appropriate cards for them without paying attention to Amazon spelling in the URL. You got the gift cards at a 20% discount sounds like a big Christmas deal, you reach the checkout page and it wants your credit or debit card details to check out, you enter the card details happily, guess who got the Christmas gift? Yes, the scammer.

They created a lookalike website for Amazon gift cards, created a fake discount page so that people could get attracted easily, and grabbed numerous card details because people ignored the n in amazon.com and then got lured into the lucrative Christmas offer. Ñ here is not the regular but called n with an accent. It is typed when you press the alt key on your keyboard with 164. It looks similar to the letter n but it is not and can easily misguide you to the wrong websites when keen attention is not paid.

How to save yourself from a lookalike website scam?

The reason we are covering this scam first is because it is the hardest to spot, but once you understand a few tricks and techniques used to execute this scam you will become pro at it.

So first, understand **Homoglyphs.**

Homoglyphs are different letters but same spelling.

For example, a lowercase "L" (l) in many fonts looks identical to a capital "i" (I), so an email sent from the address JOHN@MICROSOFT.COM would fool even the more eagle-eyed. The sender's actual address is john@mLcrosoft.com!

Some other combinations of letters look similar, for instance, **rn** looks similar to **m**, **cl** looks similar to **d**, and **vv** looks similar to **w**. All these combinations can be used to create lookalike websites, domains, or URLs.

Second, understand **combo squatting.**

Combo squatting is a website impersonation technique that hackers have been using for decades. They work because users don't check URLs for typos.

Example:	Legit website	Fake website
	Facebook.com	Facebook-secure.com
	Amazon.com	Amazon-user.com

You use legit websites every day but still, if you are routed to the fake versions of it, you might think it is the legit one and continue using it because the look and feel of the website will be the same just the URL will be different.

Third, understand **domain spoofing**.

A domain name is a unique, easy-to-remember address used to
access websites, such as 'google.com', and 'facebook.com'.

if a scammer creates a domain such as Facebook.co it will again create a similar-looking domain and people may start using it.

If you are a non-technical person concepts here might be overwhelming for you but here is the good part.

Spotting these lookalike website scams is extremely simple and you will not require any technical knowledge for that. You must have noticed that to create all these lookalike websites scammers are altering the URLs or the EMAIL addresses.

URL is the address of any website. For example, the address of Amazon's website is www.amazon.com. The URL for the Instagram website is www.instagram.com. Now whenever you want to go to a website just type in the complete URL yourself into the search bar instead of clicking any link.

If you want to go to Facebook, DO NOT TYPE FACEBOOK IN THE SEARCH BAR, INSTEAD TYPE WWW.FACEBOOK.COM IN THE ADDRESS BAR. Simple.

By doing this one simple thing you will be drowning all the efforts and money of scammers into a drain. Don't forget to do that.

Another thing you can do is to bookmark important links and websites. If you visit your bank website or cooking website daily just bookmark them, so you don't have to type it every time. You can just click on the bookmark and access your website.

If you receive an email that appears deceptive, First thoroughly check the spelling of the sender's email address, if you sense anything fishy, go to the company's official website copy their email address from there, and revert to that.

For example, if you get an email from sales@paypall.com asking for your urgent attention about a recent transaction. Check the sender's email address first, like in this scenario there is an extra "l" in PayPal which is a clear indication that this email is fake. PayPal will never send you an email with the wrong domain name in their email address.

If it is hard for you to decide if the sender's email address is correct or not, check your PayPal first whether there is a recent transaction or not. If you sense anything fishy and you want to contact PayPal then instead of replying to that email or phone number given in the email, go to the official site PayPal.com and get their email address from there and use that email address for further communication.

Here is a golden rule for you:

"Stop believing every email you receive and start obtaining information from the right channels like official websites of companies".

You will be surprised by the amount of clarity you get if you start obtaining information from the right channels.

II. Pop-up Scam:

The second kind of tech scam is a pop-up scam. The concept behind this is simple. Scammers create a fake pop-up advertisement claiming that there is a problem with your device. This fake pop-up is then deployed on websites that have big traffic, especially from elder people. As elder people are less friendly with technology, they are always the soft target. Then the scammers use pictures and logos of companies that have huge trust values like Microsoft, Apple, etc. Fake logos are easy to create but play a crucial role in authenticating the message delivered by the pop-up. Then they use this advertisement to make people call a particular number and ask for money to fix a tech problem that never existed in the first place. Let's take an example:

One fine afternoon Stacy is reading her favorite cooking website and trying to learn a new recipe for her spouse, suddenly a pop-up message appears on her screen saying her computer has been infected by harmful viruses and she needs to call this number now. Failing to do so may result in loss of data on the computer and the computer might even crash.

That message had a logo from a very reputed and trusted company Microsoft, her computer has the Microsoft operating system, and the theme, font, and color scheme everything matches Microsoft. She gets convinced and calls the number displayed on the pop-up and a person picks up the phone:

John: Thank you for calling Microsoft tech support. This is Sr. Associate, John. How can I help you?

Stacy: Hi John, this is Stacy. I got an alert on my computer that there is a virus on my computer that can delete all my data.

John: well, that's alarming mam. when did this happen?

Stacy: Just now, I was on a website looking for a cooking recipe and this message popped up.

John: Don't worry mam, we will help you to protect your data but for that first we will have to connect you with a Microsoft secure server.

Stacy: OK, but how we can do that?

John: It's very simple mam, just press the Windows key and R key on your keyboard together. You have to press both keys at the same time.

Stacy: OK, I did that and a new box appeared in front of me. It says run.

John: You did the right thing, mam. In that run box, you will see a box with "open" written in front of it. In that box type www.anydesk.com and hit enter.

Stacy: ok, it opened up a new webpage in front of me and it says smart choice for remote access.

John: that's right Stacy, and just below that you will see a button that says "Download now", click on that.

Stacy: ok it gives me a file named anydesk.exe.

John: Great, once you click on it you will get a 10-digit number mentioned as "your address". Provide me with that number so that I can connect you with a Microsoft secure server.

Stacy: ok it is 1 991 259 654.

John: all right mam, I have sent you a request from the Microsoft secure server please hit on accept on that.

Stacy: it's done.

John: well congratulations Stacy, you are now successfully connected with Microsoft and I will transfer this call to my supervisor, his name is Steve. He will help you further in diagnosing and resolving this virus situation.

Stacy: thank you John for your help.

John: My pleasure mam, if you found my assistance helpful, please give me good feedback as it helps in my promotion, I am transferring your call now.

Stacy: yes sure, I will.

Steve: Thank you for holding the line, this is Steve I am the floor supervisor. I believe I am talking to Stacy Smith.

Stacy: yes, you are.

Steve: Good afternoon Ms. Smith. How is your day today so far?

Stacy: Well, it was going good until this virus popped on my screen threatening to delete all my data.

Steve: I understand Ms. Smith. Virus situations can be frustrating and scary sometimes but you don't have to worry. As you are connected with the official support of Microsoft Windows, we will take care of this problem for you.

Stacy: ok, so what do we have to do from here?

Steve: As now you are connected with a Microsoft secure server, I will run a scan on your computer to check how severe this virus situation is and once the scan is completed, I will also help you with the solution.

Stacy: Okay.

Steve: as you can see, I have started this command prompt scan in front of you. This is an inbuilt security system given to you by Microsoft, it will scan all your computer files and once the scan is done it will display the scan results in front of us, and depending upon that we will proceed further.

Stacy: is it going to take time, because I have some cooking to do?

Steve: It would be quick Ms. Steve. As you can see on your screen, it is already done. But the results are not very positive. Can you read the last line, please?

Stacy: yes, it says, "System status hacked 5 unidentified users".

Steve: Exactly, and it is very dangerous for you. We are starting our work right away on your computer Ms. Smith. We will have to first remove all the hackers manually from your computer and then we will have to install the anti-hacking system on your device to completely protect it.

Stacy: well, that sounds complex Steve, is it going to cost me anything?

Steve: As you are already a Microsoft user, this service is free for you. We would just require some license keys to activate the product that we are providing on your computer.

Stacy: what is a license key?

Steve: A license key is a 16-digit alphanumeric code that is used as proof of ownership. We will install the product on your device which in your case is an anti-hacking system. But it will only get activated when you enter your 16-digit alphanumeric code in it.

Stacy: ok, but I don't have it.

Steve: I will instruct you how to get one. Do you have any Target stores near you?

Stacy: yes, I have one that's around 10 minutes away.

Steve: okay that's great. You can get one at Target. You just have to go to the card section of Target and you have to look for a card named "Target gift card". Once you have it just load it with $500.

Stacy: But you said that it is free.

Steve: Yes Ms. Smith, the license key and service are free for you. Once you put the card on your system and the product gets activated, exactly then we will reimburse the $500 back to the source mode of your payment which can be your credit or debit card so that you don't end up paying anything.

Stacy: I am in the middle of a cooking session, Steve. I cannot go right now; I will do it in the evening.

Steve: Ms. Smith, this is a time-sensitive matter and we cannot take any chances here. I don't know for how long I can hold the hackers from damaging your device. We are already trying our best but if you want to keep your data protected you have to get the license key as soon as possible.

Stacy: but what if I don't have $500 with me?

Steve: You can do this with your credit card as well mam or you can take help from your friends and family. As I have told you this amount will get reimbursed to you instantly. You only need these funds for 15-20 minutes.

I know that you are concerned Ms. Smith but there were 5 hackers in your device from an unknown time. They might have your bank account details, your email login, your pictures and videos stored on this computer and God knows what not. Giving them a single more minute on your device is dangerous. You need to take back control of your device ASAP.

Stacy: Alright Steve, I am on my way to Target. I will call you back with the card.

Steve: Okay Ms. Smith, if there is anyone at your house, please instruct them not to use your computer while our technicians are working on it. If the services get interrupted then we might have to restart our work and it may result in a longer time to provide you the reimbursement.

Stacy: there is no one but me, my husband will arrive in an hour.

Steve: Okay.

Stacy (after 10 minutes): Steve, I have the card is the work done?

Steve: Yes Ms. Smith. The work is done, we just need the license key numbers to activate the product. Please scratch the silver strip at the back of your card and help me with the numbers.

Stacy: it is 041-225-264-623, Access: 25875847

As she gives the numbers and pin to the hackers, she loses $500 but the scam doesn't end there. After this, the scammers will demand more gift cards and try to gain as much money as possible from Stacy. Let's take another example,

On a fine Sunday morning, Daniel decides to plan a trip with his friends. As it will be an expense, he decides to check his bank account first. Daniel turns on his computer and searches for his bank website. He is so excited about his trip that he does not check the links properly and clicks the first link that appears in front of him. This link opens a login page on his screen which is identical to his bank login page. Daniel enters his login ID and password on the login page and clicks enter which directs him to a pop-up message asking him to call his bank at "1-800-259-XXXX" as there is a security breach. The theme of this pop-up, like fonts, color scheme, and everything else matches his bank's website which he is familiar with. Assuming this is from the bank Daniel calls the number and a representative picks up the call.

Andrew: "Thank you for calling XAB bank, you are speaking with Andrew. how can I help you today?"

Daniel: Hey Andrew, my name is Daniel Webb. I was trying to log into my account when I got a message covering up my screen. The message asked me to call this number as there was a security breach.

Andrew: To confirm the security breach, I will first have to verify your identity sir. Please help me with the last four of your account number.

Daniel: the last four is 4568.

Andrew: Yes Mr. Webb. As I can see here your account status is hacked. Due to the same reason, we have kept one of your transactions on hold which was initiated today at 10 in the morning.

Daniel: But I have not initiated any transaction. Which transaction are you talking about?

Andrew: We have received a request for a wire transfer for the amount of $11000 to be processed in a Canadian bank account ending in 5582.

Daniel: No, I have not done that. Someone is trying to rob me by entering my account. I request you to cancel that transfer immediately.

Andrew: I am afraid Mr. Webb; we cannot make any changes to your account as it has been hacked. To make any changes first we will have to secure your account. As this is a very serious matter, I am transferring your call to my manager, Mary. She will help you to secure your account first and after that, we will cancel this transaction.

Daniel: OK, please do it quickly.

Mary: Thank you for holding the line. You are speaking with Mary I manage the customer interactions team. Am I speaking with Mr. Webb?

Daniel: Yes, you are. My account is really important to me and I want to protect it ASAP.

Mary: I understand your concern Mr. Webb and I will help you to do it in the shortest time possible. To secure your account you will have to go to your bank first. Can you give me an approximate time in which you will reach your bank?

Daniel: I would require at least 15 to 20 minutes to reach there.

Mary: OK Daniel, please do that and call me back before going inside the bank. It is very important as I will have to provide you with a few specific instructions to secure your account. Without those instructions, your account may get frozen which would become a bigger problem for you.

And Daniel as this matter is under investigation from the bank's side, I would appreciate it if you could keep this thing to yourself only, and not discuss this hacking situation with anyone else.

Daniel: Okay I am on my way. I will call you on the same number when I reach the bank.

Daniel (after 15 minutes): Hello, I need to speak with Mary. I am outside the bank.

Mary: yes, Daniel. You are speaking with Mary. As I can see currently your account status is hacked and to protect your funds, we will have to transfer your funds into a secure account and we will have to terminate your current account.

Daniel: Does that mean that I have to open a new account?

Mary: No Daniel. Your identity is red-flagged due to the hacking activity and for the same reason you cannot open a new account.
We were already familiar with this situation and that is the reason we have arranged a safe account for you to secure your funds.

Daniel: I would be more comfortable to transfer the funds into my wife's account.

Mary: As hackers have complete control of your account Daniel, transferring funds into your wife's account would be a bad idea as it would put her account at risk as well. We have created a dummy account for you which you can safely use for 48 hours. Do you have a pen and paper to write the information down?

Daniel: Yes, go ahead.

Mary:

    Account Name: Richard Hendricks
    Account Number: 589622564177
    Account routing: 1478522580
    Bank name: DDFC Bank
    Amount: $19000

Once you go inside, just tell the teller that you want to make a domestic wire transfer and give them these details. If they ask you the reason for the transfer just tell them that there is a medical emergency in your friends' family and you want the funds to be cleared ASAP.

Daniel: I am very uncomfortable with this Mary. This is my life's savings and cannot take any risk with that.

Mary: If you go and tell the bank about the hacking activity, they will freeze your account right away Mr. Webb. As I can see in your account, your mortgage is due in 3 days and there are other bills to pay. You are currently not in a situation to live without your account even for a single day and that's why we are helping you with this solution.

Daniel: But why should I trust you? You may be the hacker who is trying to get my funds.

Mary: haha (laughs in an insensitive manner). Daniel, we have your complete account details, we have your Internet banking login ID and password. We can even see your recent transactions and upcoming bills. This is sufficient information to make any transfer online without your consent. If we wanted your money, we could have just transferred it into an offshore account, without even making you aware of it. My point is that we don't have to send you to a bank and give you an account number for this, we can do it online. But our intention is not to rob you instead we are trying to protect you here.

Daniel, we are not the bad guys here. Our conversation from the beginning is getting recorded and if I give you any wrong instructions, I will not only lose my job but also there will be a federal inquiry against me. I have a family that I love Daniel and just for your $19000, I am not committing any crime that will separate me from them. So, without wasting a single minute proceed further and protect your funds also take the receipt of the transfer once done.

Daniel: OK Mary, I am trusting you on this. But if this thing doesn't work out, I am going to the police station where my friend works.

Mary: you are getting worried about the wrong person Mr. Webb. You should be worried about the hackers who are trying to steal $11000 from your account. We are the ones protecting you. It is a time-sensitive matter, Mr. Webb, Please hurry up.

Daniel: Okay, I will be back in a couple of minutes.

Daniel (after 20 minutes): Mary, the transfer is done and I have the receipt.

Mary: Okay Mr. Webb. Please email a copy of the receipt to Maryjohnson@gmail.XXX.

Daniel: Okay it is done. Now how can I get this money back?

Mary: The cooling off time for wire transfer is 24 working hours Mr. Webb. So please stay on the line with us we are doing the paperwork on your case.

Scammers will keep Daniel engaged on call for the whole day. The maximum time to complete the transfer is 24 hours but it gets completed before that as well. Sometimes in 4-5 hours also. As soon as money hits the receiver's bank account it will be withdrawn instantly and Daniel will lose all his life savings.

Protection tips from pop-up scams:

If you observe the pattern of a pop-up scam, they first want to grab your attention by flashing a concerning or exciting advertisement on your computer, which is nothing but triggering an emotion of fear in you. Like a virus is in your computer or your data is at risk.

Once they do that, the next thing they want is your trust. They will use brands and logos that have trust value like Amazon, Microsoft, and any popular bank like BOA, Wells Fargo, etc. They want you to feel things not understand things and for that trust is required.

Once they know that they have your trust, they will quickly create an urgency because if they give you the time, two things can happen that will ruin their scam. The first thing is if they give you time you will rethink and reanalyze the whole situation and you may make decisions with your independent thinking which might not go in their favor. The second thing is you may discuss this situation with any third person like your family, friend, lawyer, or any other person who can stop you from making the wrong decision in the spur of the moment.

If they have to make you talk to someone like a cab driver, store representative, or bank person, they will always ask you to keep this thing private and confidential. By maintaining secrecy in the scam, they make you believe that all other people apart from the scammer can harm you and you need to keep everything private until the scammer gets the money.

Finally, the loopholes, transferring funds to an unknown bank account, and buying gift cards are all loopholes in the system. Which can be used and manipulated to rob people.

The golden trick to protect yourself from the pop-up scam is to obtain information from the right channels. If you have a pop-up from the bank claiming there is a security breach, call the number on your credit/debit card or call the number on your chequebook to obtain information. If you don't have the number to your bank then go to the bank and talk to someone in person. Never call the number that is displayed on the pop-up advertisement claiming to be from your bank or any other company that you work with.

If you have a pop-up from tech companies like Amazon or Microsoft and you don't know which number to call, take time to do your research, call people, and discuss with them. Don't let the trigger of fear or greed compel you to make a nasty decision. Take your time and act wisely. If you still cannot figure it out just go to your local technician. Your instant decision from the trigger of fear or greed is the fire starter. Do not take action based on this trigger. *Remind yourself that you are the one in control, not the scammer.*

III. Cold calling tech support scam:

It is the old school cold calling scam which is very effective. The beauty of this scam is it does not use any tech tricks like in the above two scams but a golden script that reels in the prospect. The efficiency of this scam lies in its simplicity and a virus trick. So, follow this one carefully.

The scammer first chooses a legit company name to call you like Microsoft, Google, Bing, windows, Comcast, Verizon, etc. Once the name is locked, they will cold call you out of the blue telling you that they are receiving "security threats" or "error signals" or "trojan warning" from your device, basically anything that triggers a fear emotion.

Then they will show you some errors and warnings on your computer and project them as viruses. Then they will charge you money to remove them. Let's understand it with an example:

On a fine Sunday morning, Jacob is getting ready for a fishing trip. He is thrilled because he is catching up with his childhood friends after a long time. He was just about to leave when his phone rang.

Gary: Hello this is Gary calling you from Microsoft tech support. Am I speaking with Jacob Henderson?

Jacob: yes. What is the purpose of your call?

Gary: Mr. Henderson, we have been receiving some error messages from your computer for the last few weeks. When we decoded these messages, we discovered that some trojan viruses were getting installed on your device. These viruses are harmful enough to damage your device and have the potential to send your data to foreign hackers. These viruses are the reason we gave you a call today.

Jacob: this sounds fishy. My computer is working fine and I have no problem with it.

Gary: Mr. Henderson, the viruses that I am talking about are stored in the computer management part of your device. You are not aware of those viruses because either you are not using an antivirus or your anti-virus is not able to detect those viruses, both of them are very harmful situations.

Jacob: I get a lot of calls like these every day and I know that all you people want is to access my computer remotely. I am not falling for your trap.

Gary: Mr. Henderson, we have no interest in accessing your computer remotely. Our job is to show you the viruses and help you delete them so that you can protect your data and device. We just need 5 minutes of your time and nothing else.

Give it a chance and if you don't feel good about it you can hang up after five minutes.

Jacob: All alright, go ahead.

Gary: there are only two objectives here sir, The first is to locate the viruses and the second is to delete them. Are you in front of your computer?

Jacob: No, I am on my way out. Give me a moment.

Gary: Alright sir, when you are in front of the computer just press the Windows key with the "R" key. You have to press both keys together.

Jacob: ok, it brings up a new box in front of me that says Run.

Gary: Great. In that box clear the bar that says open and type in "eventvwr" and hit enter.

Jacob: ok, it brings up another window that says event viewer.

Gary: that's right Mr. Henderson. This event viewer is a part of computer management which is the most important part of the computer. This event viewer window is the part where hackers have strategically stored viruses to gain access to your data.

Jacob: but it looks like a normal window with some information in it, there are no viruses here.

Gary: the viruses are hidden inside sir. At the left of the window make a double left click on custom view.

Jacob: Okay.

Gary: Now below the custom view option there is "administrative events", as soon as you click on it all the viruses will appear in front of you.

Jacob: oh no, there is a whole bunch of them, but they are not showing up as viruses.

Gary: yes Mr. Henderson they are showing up as errors and warnings because they are not normal viruses, they are harmful trojan viruses that are specially designed in such a way that they remain undetected from anti-virus software and can transfer important information of your computer to the hackers.

Jacob: So, how should we delete them?

Gary: The good part here is deleting these viruses is very easy. Just make a right click on any one of them and hit the delete option.

Jacob: I am not getting any delete option.

Gary: when you make a right-click on any virus you will get options like event properties, attach task, copy, save, refresh, help, and delete. You have to click on the delete option.

Jacob: I am getting all the above options but I am not getting any delete.

Gary: ok, well that is unusual but still what you can do is you can just select one of them by making a left click on them and once the virus is highlighted in blue color you can hit the delete key from your keyboard.

Jacob: I am doing that. I am hitting the delete key continuously but the virus is not getting deleted.

Gary: can you tell me sir what is the number of events written at the top of this list?

Jacob: The number of events is more than 6000.

Gary: oh no Mr. Henderson. I believe the virus infection has reached such a critical level that it has corrupted your delete option. I am afraid that I will not be able to help you further if the delete option is corrupted.

Jacob: So, what should I do? Get a new anti-virus?

Gary: no sir. It will not help as the infection has already spread in your computer and it is highly possible that till now your identity has been stolen. The best thing I can do for you in this situation is I can connect your device to a Windows secure server and I can transfer your call to a Microsoft-certified senior technician. I am sure you can get some help from there.

Jacob: Okay.

Gary: Just press the windows key and the letter "R" key together at the same time.

Jacob: I again see the run box in front of me.

Gary: yes Mr. Henderson. In that box, clear the bar that says open and then type in www.teamviewer.com and press enter.

Jacob: OK, it brings me to a new TeamViewer page that says free download.

Gary: yes sir, click on the free download option and then install the downloaded file, once done let me know.

Jacob: installation is done now it is giving me an ID and a password.

Gary: yes, please help me with those details.

Jacob:

        ID:1-758-965-857
        Password: Xc5894

Gary: I have sent you a connection request from the Windows secure server, please accept it.

Jacob: Okay it's done.

Gary: Mr. Henderson now you are successfully connected with a Windows secure server I am transferring your call now to our Microsoft-certified senior technician. His name is Brandon. We have already briefed him about your case and he will help you to secure your device and data from the hackers.

Jacob: Thank you, Gary. I am looking forward to talk to him.

Brandon: Thank you for holding the line, I believe I am talking to Mr. Jacob Henderson.

Jacob: yes, you are.

Brandon: Hello Mr. Henderson. How is your day today so far?

Jacob: it was going well until I got this call. Now, I am really worried about my data and identity.

Brandon: I understand Mr. Henderson that getting this kind of call can make people concerned about their device security. But the good part is that now at least you are aware of the problem and we are here to help you solve it.

Jacob: All the scanned copies of my IDs are saved on this device which makes me concerned. This virus situation is both confusing and frustrating. Can you remove them from my device?

Brandon: Yes Mr. Henderson. I will help you in doing that. As you can see, I am starting a command prompt scan on your device. Command prompt is a Windows original software that you can use to scan your device. Based on this scan results we will take action to remove the viruses from your device.

Jacob: Is it going to take a long time as I have a meeting to attend?

Brandon: Not much sir, 2 to 3 minutes max.

Jacob: Okay.

Brandon: the scan is done, sir. In this command prompt window, the last line is the scan result. Can you read that?

Jacob: yes, it says "system status hacked. Identity compromised. Unknown users found"

Brandon: that's right sir. It is a very critical situation. Before we proceed further, I want to know if you use this device for entertainment purposes only like watching movies playing games, etc., or if you do online banking and shopping also.

Jacob: I do online banking.

Brandon: Mr. Henderson, in that situation we have to install an anti-hacking software immediately on your device. First, we will remove these unknown users manually from your device and then we will move towards the viruses.

Jacob: yes, I agree to act immediately. I cannot risk losing my identity. My brother has faced identity theft in the past and I know how troublesome that situation is.

Brandon: that's right Mr. Henderson. Identity theft is a nightmare. We have already started our work on your device. As you are an existing user of Microsoft the services are free for you but the software, we are providing you will require a product license key.

Jacob: What is a license key?

Brandon: It is used as proof of ownership. You can easily get it at Walmart.

Jacob: ok, Walmart is close to me, I can ask them for a Microsoft license key.

Brandon: Sir, as Walmart is a third-party store, they will not be aware of the term "license key". You will have to ask them for a "Walmart money card". To make things simple and ensure that you don't end up making a mistake I will stay on the line with you. Once you park at the parking lot of Walmart just say hello to me. I will guide you further.

Jacob: I don't know why this thing is so complicated. I am on my way. Tell me which card I have to get.

Brandon: once you go inside the store you will see a section of cards where different kinds of cards will be placed. From that bunch pick a card that says Walmart money card, take it to the cashier, and load $500 on it. Once you have it just let me know. If anyone asks you why you need the card, just tell them it is for your personal use.

Jacob: I can't believe I am doing this. I just want this thing to end ASAP.

Brandon: trust me Mr. Henderson you are doing the right thing you just have to take care of the card, for everything else you can count on us. We have already removed the unknown users from your device and till the time you get the card remaining three will be removed as well.

Jacob: hang on I am going inside.

Brandon: okay sir you can keep the phone in your pocket, let me know when you are out of the store.

Jacob (After some time): Brandon I have the card for you.

Brandon: please scratch the backside of the card sir and help me with the 16-digit numbers.

Jacob: 5698-5874-1526-3511

And that's how Jacob got scammed. As you already know till now that the scam does not end there. They will try to take as much money from victims as possible.

Protection tips from cold-calling tech support scams.

As you may have learned in the first two variations of tech scams, protecting yourself becomes very easy if you know what exactly is happening. Most people get scammed because of a lack of knowledge about scam psychology and their way of operation. Now the golden trick for protecting yourself from cold calling tech support scams, which we have discussed before as well is: *"To receive information from the right channels and via the right means of communication"*.

Apart from this golden rule, you can also do the following things:

Ask for a written form of communication:
If you get a call out of the blue, telling you that the computer is infected, in this situation just ask them to send you an email. If they do not have your email ID just hang up and block the number. Companies like Microsoft, Verizon, and other big companies will always have your email address if you are their customer.

Check for tampered spellings:

If they send you an email always look for the sender's email address. Look for combo squatting or domain spoofing as we have learned earlier in this book. If you find it fake, just mark it as spam and report it to Google.

Talk to people:
Still, if you have any confusion, consult your local technicians or any friend or family member who is better at tech.

Refuse gift card payments:
If they demand money in gift cards just hang up and block the number, legit companies will always have better and more trustworthy payment options for you like credit and debit card options or PayPal.

Do not allow remote access:
In tech scams, the scammers will always try to gain remote access to your device. It can be your computer, tablet, or cell phone. Do not allow remote access to your device to anyone that you don't know.

By following the above steps, you can destroy the scammer's attempts, time, and money and you can protect yourself from cold-calling tech support scams.

IV. BSOD Scam.

So, once we have learned about the first three kinds of tech scams, it is time now to understand the fourth one which is the "BLUE SCREEN OF DEATH" scam. This is a more advanced tech scam where scammers and social engineers use technology to disable your access to your computer. Your keyboard and mouse stop working and even if you restart the computer the situation does not change and you are left with no other option other than calling the number displayed on the screen.

"BLUE SCREEN OF DEATH", is a genuine Microsoft error, but scammers have created a BSOD scam using it. They try to send you a malicious file and once the malicious file executes, it creates a fake BSOD experience by hiding the cursor and disabling Task Manager, both of which create the impression that the system is not responding. It also displays a message that instructs you to call them back, like:

"If you would like to resolve the issue, please reach out to our support team immediately at 1-800-418-XXXX."

Genuine Blue Screens of Death scenarios do not contain any such sentences or phone numbers.

Fake BSOD is a product of social engineering, and it can be executed in a couple of different ways for example: BSOD porn, BSOD banking, BSOD Microsoft, or BSOD Windows etc.

BSOD porn appears on porn websites, and it tells you that you have violated federal law and there are charges pressed against you, they will disable your mouse and keyboard and you will not be able to close that screen. There will be a number to call on that screen, you call that number and on the other side a person will be ready with a script to scam you.

BSOD banking appears when you are surfing your bank website or any other bank website, it will disable your controls and display a concerning message on screen. Like "bank security compromised" or anything that triggers a fear emotion and there will be a number to call.

BSOD Microsoft or BSOD Windows will pop up a similar blue screen in front of you displaying an error message regarding your operating system or system failure and will also have a callback number. Let's take an example:

On one fine afternoon, Frank's daughter called him up asking for help with her tuition fee. He had money saved up and told her that he was transferring funds for her tuition fee right away. He picks up his laptop and searches for his bank name on Google. Without paying attention he clicks the first link that appears in front of him. The scammers have created this fake lookalike website of his bank. It looks identical to the one he is looking for and as he clicks the link, he gets a new page with a green button saying proceed to login. This was something new to him but as it was saying proceed to login, he clicked that. This link downloaded an executable file on his device which is specifically designed to infect the Windows operating system. But as it got downloaded from the bank's website and got saved as "your account info", he thought it was from the bank and might contain some important information, as soon as he clicked it, a code was activated which is similar to a virus.

It did four things to Frank's computer:

> Made his laptop screen blue hiding the closing and minimizing options at the right top.

> Made his mouse pointer disappear, which gave him a false feeling that his mouse was not working.

> A text starts typing itself on the computer stating *"Your banking security is compromised, call our support team immediately at 1800-465-XXXX"*.

> A voice from his laptop starts repeating the message written on the screen on a loop.

This gimmick of social engineering is designed to make people strongly believe that something is wrong with their computers and to trigger a strong emotion of fear in them. The most common option that people opt for in these situations is to call the number displayed on the screen. Frank does the same thing, when he calls the number displayed on the screen a person picks up the phone and starts talking.

Dennis: Thank you for calling DCD bank, how can I help you?

Frank: I was trying to visit the bank's website when suddenly my computer stopped working, the screen became blue and a message came up saying my banking security is compromised. This number was mentioned on the screen to call.

Dennis: Okay sir, I want to inform you that this situation takes place when there is a hacking attack on your computer. Whenever the hackers try to get to your internet banking to make any fraudulent transfers our cloud security system locks down your computer to protect your funds.

Frank: Okay, does that mean that my funds are still protected?

Dennis: To provide you with more information I would first need to verify some of your information, sir. Please provide me with your first and last name and the last four digits of your account number.

Frank: My name is Frank Marshal and the last four of my account are 3359.

Dennis: Thank you for the information, Mr. Marshal. As I can see there were three attempts made to transfer funds from this account but the bank security has denied all the attempts due to the involvement of a suspicious IP address which was from Russia.

Frank: what does that mean?

Dennis: Every computer has an IP address sir which is a combination of a bunch of numbers that tell us where the computer is located and who is the internet service provider for that computer.

Frank: OK.

Dennis: We verify numerous details before processing a wire transfer that includes verification of IP address as well. Yesterday three attempts were made from your account ending with 3359 to transfer funds into an offshore account. In our verification process, the IP address from which this wire transfer request was made was from Moscow in Russia. It was a big red flag for us and due to the same reason, we canceled the transactions.

Frank: Oh, thank you so much. I want to inform you that I never attempted any wire transfer yesterday. It seems my account is hacked. What should I do to protect it? and also my computer is stuck at this blue screen.

Dennis: We will help you Mr. Marshal to come out of this hacker situation. You just have to follow our instructions step by step. Are you in front of your computer?

Frank: yes, I am.

Dennis: okay try pressing the key combination which is the Windows key and the letter "L" and tell me if you see any changes on your screen.

Frank: No, I am pressing Windows and L at the same time but the screen is still the same.

Dennis: okay, try pressing alt and tab together.

Frank: No, it is not working either.

Dennis: try, pressing Windows + alt + D.

Frank: Okay, it worked. I am back at my screen.

Dennis: great, but do not click anywhere else and don't press any button until I tell you to, or else you will come back to the blue screen.

Frank: Okay, I see my bank website in Google Chrome.

Dennis: use your mouse to close all the open windows and return to your desktop screen.

Frank: ok, done.

Dennis: now press the windows key with the letter R.

Frank: Okay it brings a new box in front of me that says run.

Dennis: Great, now clear the bar that says open and type in www.teamviewer.com and hit enter.

Frank: ok I just did that and it opened a new web page in front of me.

Dennis: That's the TeamViewer home page, Mr. Marshal. On that page click on the download button.

Frank: ok as I clicked on download it gave me a new file that says TeamViewer.exe.

Dennis: Yes, that's right sir, install this file on your computer and let me know once you are done.

Frank: It is installed and it is giving me an ID and a password.

Dennis: Great. Provide me the ID and the password.

Frank:

                ID: 1 568 951 247
                Password: 75895

Dennis: I have sent you a request to connect you with our secure server. Please hit accept on that notification.

Frank: okay, it's done.

Dennis: Mr. Marshal, now you are successfully connected with our bank server and I can see that the hackers are still active on your device. There are 3 hackers from different locations.

Frank: can you remove them?

Dennis: Yes. But it will take time. The right thing to do in this situation is to first secure your account so that your funds stay protected and then we go behind the hackers.

Frank: well, yes that sounds right to me.

Dennis: The only challenge we have here is that is it dangerous to protect your account while the hackers are monitoring our activity. To deviate their attention. We will make your screen blank for 5-10 minutes. That's the approximate time to secure your account.

Frank: I don't think I understand it, but that is fine. My primary objective right now is to get rid of the hackers.

Dennis: I have opened your internet banking login screen which ended in a blue screen last time. I have fixed the blue screen issue. You go ahead now and log in to your account.

Frank: okay it's done.

Dennis: now I am making the screen black so that the hackers don't see your account.

(at this point Dennis activates the black screen feature available in remote support software so that Frank cannot see what is happening on his account).

Frank: okay, I cannot see anything now.

Dennis: it is only for 5-10 minutes; things will be back to normal once the account is secure. We are generating a one-time password that you will receive on your phone to secure your balance which is $9586 at this moment.

Frank: Okay.

Dennis: once you receive it let me know.

Frank: yes, I received it. It is 885971.

Dennis: Well, Congratulations Mr. Marshal. Your account is now secured and now we are starting the process to remove the hackers it will take at least 24 hours.

Frank: What the Hell! I just got a message that my wire transfer of $9586 is completed.

Dennis: This is a self-wire transfer, Mr. Marshal. You can relax. The funds are in your account only and will be accessible to you in approximately 24 hours' time.

Frank: but 24 hours is too long. What is If need the funds before that?

Dennis: We have told you the maximum time Dennis. It is also possible that it will be done in the next 2 hours. We will try our best to do it as soon as possible.

In this scam scenario, Dennis's main task was to complete the wire transfer. Now his next task is to hold Frank for the next 24 working hours so that the funds get reflected in his desired bank account. 24 hours is the maximum time it can get done sooner as well.

Usually, the scammer in these cases will have co-workers who will talk to the victim one by one acting as bank managers, police officers, better business bureau representatives, etcetera. They will speak to the victim with the following objectives:

> Calm down the victim
> Gain the victim's trust and make him comfortable.
> Strech conversation as much as possible
> Waste the victim's time till the wire transfer gets cleared.

As soon as the wire transfer is reflected in the receiver's bank account, they will hang up the call and the victim will be scammed.

How to protect yourself from BSOD scams?

Recognize the Scam: Be aware that legitimate error messages from your operating system will not include a phone number to call for support. Understand that reputable companies, like Microsoft, will not contact you unsolicited to inform you of computer issues.

Do Not Call the Number: Never call the phone number provided on the fake error screen. This is a tactic used by scammers to gain access to your computer or trick you into paying for unnecessary services. Call the customer care number of Microsoft or shoot them an email. If required take the help of any local technician but do not call the number displayed on the screen.

Avoid Remote Access: Do not grant remote access to your computer to anyone who contacts you out of the blue, especially if you did not initiate the support request.

Enable Pop-Up Blockers: Use browser settings or extensions to block pop-ups. Many tech support scams are initiated through pop-up messages on malicious websites.

Educate Yourself: Stay informed about common scams and phishing tactics. Be skeptical of unexpected calls, pop-ups, or emails claiming urgent issues with your computer.

D. Job Offer scams:

Job offer scams are prevalent in the online job market, where fraudsters pose as legitimate employers offering high-paying jobs in exchange for personal information or upfront fees. These scams often target individuals seeking work-from-home opportunities and promise high salaries with minimal effort. Victims may end up providing sensitive information such as social security numbers or paying upfront fees, only to realize the job offer was fake. Let us understand the execution of this scam with this example.

Martha is a young girl who just passed college and is looking for job opportunities. She was scrolling through her email when she suddenly saw a new email with thrilling news.

> Subject: Exciting Work-From-Home Opportunity - Immediate Hiring!
>
> Dear Martha,
>
> We hope this email finds you well. We came across your resume on LinkedIn and were impressed with your

qualifications. Our company, social Innovations, is currently looking for motivated individuals to join our team for an exciting work-from-home opportunity.

> Position: Online Marketing Associate
> Location: Remote
> Salary: $3,000 - $5,000 per month (based on performance)

Job Description:

As an Online Marketing Associate, you will be responsible for promoting our cutting-edge products and services through various online channels. Your tasks will include social media marketing, email campaigns, and search engine optimization. No prior experience is required as full training will be provided.

Requirements:

- High school diploma or equivalent
- Basic computer skills
- Strong communication skills
- Ability to work independently

Benefits:

- Flexible working hours
- Work from the comfort of your own home
- Competitive monthly salary
- Performance-based bonuses

> To apply, simply reply to this email with your updated resume and a brief cover letter explaining why you are the ideal candidate for this position.
>
> Please note that this is a time-sensitive opportunity, and we are looking to fill the position quickly.

Now once you fill in the details and submit your resume, someone will call you back from this company.

Martha gets a call a day after replying to the email.

Steve: Hello Martha, this is Steve calling you from Social Innovations, how are you doing today?

Martha: I am doing good Steve. Thank you for asking.

Steve: We are delighted to tell you that we have short-listed your job application for the online marketing associate post.

Martha: Well, that's great. I am excited about this new job opportunity.

Steve: We would like to work with you Martha but before we can schedule your final interview call with our HR manager, we need to verify your identity. It is required because after the invention of AI technology and chat GPT lot of people are submitting multiple fake resumes to increase their chances of getting a job.

Martha: oh, that's so disheartening to hear. I can assure you that I have not done anything like that. I am ok to go through identity verification.

Steve: I appreciate your co-operation, Martha. I will ask you a few questions on this recorded line and you have to answer them in the least words possible. Are you ready?

Martha: Yes, let's get this thing done.

Steve: please state your complete name as mentioned in your state ID.

Martha: Martha S Stevens.

Steve: Mention your cell phone number for further communications.

Martha: 819-256-XXXX.

Steve: Mention your previous work experience.

Martha: I have an internship experience with college in managing social media accounts and I am a first-time job aspirant.

Steve: OK, for age and ID verification, please state your DOB and SSN.

Martha: it's 24/01/2001 and 5589.

Steve: Thank you, Martha. Our company has a policy of crediting salaries directly into the accounts which is done biweekly. Do you have any checking or savings accounts?

Martha: Yes, I have savings.

Steve: That's great Martha, which bank do you bank with? And what are the last four of your accounts?

Martha: It is the Bank of America with 3369.

Steve: Thank you, Martha. The verification is complete now. I am transferring you to our HR manager Danny Johnson. Mr. Johnson will take the final round of interviews. Your verification is complete and I wish you the best of luck for your final round. Thank you.

Martha: Thank you, Steve. It was a pleasure talking to you.

Danny: Good morning, Martha. Thank you for joining us today. How are you?

Martha: Good morning, Danny. I'm doing well, thank you. I am excited for the opportunity to discuss the Online Marketing Associate position.

Danny: Absolutely, and we're thrilled to have you here. Let's start the interview. Can you tell us about your background and experience in online marketing?

Martha: Certainly. I have a Bachelor's degree in Marketing and have a six-month internship experience in managing social media accounts. My experience includes managing social media campaigns, developing content strategies, and optimizing websites for better visibility.

Danny: Great. Your resume indicates a solid foundation. Could you share an example of a successful online marketing campaign you've led in the past?

Martha: Certainly. In my previous role as an Intern, I spearheaded a social media campaign that resulted in a 30% increase in brand awareness and a 20% boost in online sales within two months. We utilized targeted ads and engaged with the audience through interactive content, generating a positive response.

Danny: That sounds impressive, Martha. Moving on, our Online Marketing Associates often work independently. How do you manage your time and stay motivated when working remotely?

Martha: I've experienced working remotely, and I understand the importance of discipline and organization. I use project management tools to set clear goals, prioritize tasks, and ensure timely delivery. Regular check-ins with the team also help maintain motivation and collaboration.

Danny: Good to know. Adaptability is crucial, especially in a remote setting. Can you share your experience with adapting to new tools or platforms for marketing purposes?

Martha: Absolutely. In my previous role, we frequently adopted new tools and platforms to stay ahead in the dynamic landscape. I'm familiar with various analytics tools, social media management platforms, and CRM systems. I enjoy exploring and mastering new technologies to enhance marketing strategies.

Danny: That's a valuable skill. One final question, Martha. What do you think sets you apart from other candidates, and why do you believe you would be a great fit for the Online Marketing Associate role at Social Innovations?

Martha: I believe my combination of hands-on experience, strategic thinking, and adaptability sets me apart. I am passionate about staying current with industry trends, and I'm confident in my ability to contribute to Social Innovations' marketing objectives through innovative and effective strategies.

Danny: Thank you, Martha. It was a pleasure getting to know more about your experiences and skills. We'll be in touch soon regarding the next steps in the hiring process.

Martha: Thank you, Danny. I appreciate the opportunity and look forward to the possibility of joining the Social Innovations team.

After 8 hours of the interview, Martha receives an email.

Subject: Congratulations on Your Successful Interview with Social Innovations!

Dear Martha,

I hope this email finds you well. I am delighted to extend my heartfelt congratulations to you for successfully clearing the interview for the Online Marketing Associate position at Social Innovations!

Your impressive background, experience, and enthusiasm for the role truly stood out during the interview. The hiring team was particularly impressed with your accomplishments in leading successful online marketing campaigns and your proactive approach to staying current with industry trends.

We are excited about the possibility of having you on board, and we will be in touch soon with more details regarding the next steps in the hiring process. Please share with us a copy of the following documents so that we can start your enrollment process.

1. Front and back of your driver's license.
2. A copy of your passport.
3. Certificate of your educational qualifications.
4. A $200 payment as a document processing fee on a green dot visa card, which will be reimbursed with your first salary.

Once again, congratulations on this significant achievement. We look forward to the prospect of welcoming you to our team and achieving great success together.

If you have any questions or need further information, please feel free to reach out.

Best regards,
Danny Johnson
HR Manager
Social Innovations

After receiving this email Martha is at the peak of her happiness. In a shortening economy where people are losing jobs, she has managed to obtain one, and that too in her first interview. A feeling of pride and confidence is rushing through her body. She quickly clicks a picture of her driver's license, passport, and educational certificates gets a green dot card from her nearest store, and sends them by email.

She got scammed the moment she sent the email. These kinds of job offer scams are getting quite popular and increasing day by day and this is the level of professionalism scammers follow to trap you. Follow the given red flags to detect and eliminate such kind of scam attempts.

*(social innovation is a made-up name to better explain this example)

Red flags to look out for in Job Offer Scams:

Too Good to Be True Salary: Scammers often lure victims with high salaries for positions that typically pay much less.

Very quick Interview Process: Legitimate companies conduct interviews to assess candidate's suitability for the role. If a job is offered with a quick interview, it is a big Red Flag.

Unprofessional Email Address: Check the email address of the sender. Legitimate companies use professional email addresses associated with their domain.

Request for Payment: Legitimate employers will never ask you to pay for job opportunities. If they request payment for training materials or other expenses, it's likely a scam.

Ask for too much documentation via email or phone: Legitimate companies always ask you to submit documents in their office to an employee in person, not over the phone or email.

E. Lottery Scams:

Lottery scams involve fake notifications claiming that the recipient has won a large sum of money in a lottery or sweepstakes. To claim the prize, victims are required to pay taxes or processing fees, which the scammers pocket before disappearing. These scams often target vulnerable individuals seeking financial security and can lead to significant financial losses. Example:

Steve received an email notification on his computer and opened it.

Subject: Congratulations! You've Won the Global Jackpot Lottery - Claim Your $1,00,000 Prize Now!

Dear Steve,

We are thrilled to inform you that your email address has been randomly selected as the grand prize winner in our prestigious Global Jackpot Lottery! This is a momentous occasion, and we extend our warmest congratulations to you on becoming the fortunate recipient of a staggering USD 1,00,000.

To facilitate the smooth processing of your winnings, kindly follow the instructions below:

Step 1: Provide Information

To ensure a seamless transfer of your prize money, we require the following details:

Full Name

Residential Address

Date of Birth

Occupation

Step 2: Bank Account Details

For a secure and swift transfer, please share your bank account details, including:

Bank Name

Account Number

Routing Number

Step 3: Processing Fee Payment

To cover administrative costs and applicable taxes, there is a nominal processing fee of $200. This can be paid through any of the following methods:

Wire Transfer:

Credit Card

PayPal

Upon completing these steps, your $1,00,000 prize will be promptly transferred to your provided bank account.

Important Notes:

Please treat this communication with the utmost confidentiality to avoid any unauthorized access to your winnings.

The processing fee is a one-time payment and ensures the swift and secure transfer of your prize.

We urge you to act promptly to claim your prize before the specified deadline.

Contact Information:

For any inquiries or assistance, feel free to contact me at [201-225-XXXX].

Congratulations once again on your remarkable win, and we look forward to disbursing your well-deserved prize money!

Best Regards,

John Smith

Global Lottery Coordinator

Steve in excitement sends his credit card details to process a payment of $200 and gets scammed for a much larger amount.

$100,000 can be a life-changing amount for anyone. When victims receive this kind of email, they get excited and their wishful thinking compels them to send money and personal information to scammers. A $200 fee to process a $100,000 lottery amount sounds like a very minimal downside for a huge return, that's why they fall victim to such scams. What people fail to understand is that their data is precious and they must not share it with people online no matter how big the bait is.

Red Flags to spot a lottery scam:

Unsolicited communication: You didn't participate in any lottery, yet you're being informed of a win.

Personal information request: Legitimate lotteries don't ask for sensitive information like full name, address, and bank details via email.

Processing fee: Legitimate lotteries don't require winners to pay upfront fees to claim prizes.

Pressure tactics: Urgency is created to prompt quick action, a common strategy in scams.

Generic sender details: Lack of specific information about the lottery organization or contact details raises suspicion.

F. Flight Booking Scam:

Flight booking scams typically involve fake travel websites offering steep discounts on airline tickets. Victims may book flights through these websites, only to receive fake confirmation emails or no tickets. In some cases, scammers use stolen credit card information to book flights, leaving victims liable for fraudulent transactions. Example:

Jenny, excited about her upcoming vacation, begins searching online for affordable airline tickets. While browsing, she stumbles upon a Google ad claiming to offer incredible discounts. The ad displays a phone number, urging potential customers to call for exclusive deals.

Intrigued by the promise of heavy discounts, Jenny decides to call the provided number.

Jenny: Hello, is this the number for the exclusive airline discounts?

Joseph (Warmly): Yes, indeed! You've reached the right place. This is Joseph, and I'm here to help you secure fantastic discounts on your flight bookings. May I have your name, please?

Jenny: I'm Jenny. I saw your ad online, and I'm interested in booking a flight at a discount.

Joseph: Great to have you, Jenny! We have some amazing deals available right now. To get started, could you please provide me with your full name and address?

Jenny: Sure, it's Jenny Thompson, and I live at 123 Pine Street Portland Oregon.

Joseph: Thank you, Jenny. Now, let's select the perfect flight for you. Can you share your preferred travel dates and destination?

Jenny: I'm planning to fly to Washington DC on the 15th of next month and return on the 22nd.

Joseph: Okay, and you plan to book a stay as well or just the flight?

Jenny: I called you to book a flight, but if you can get me some good options for a stay, I can be interested.

Joseph: Excellent choice Jenny! As we are official partners of American Airlines and travel partners with the best hotels in Washington DC, I am very confident that we can give some really good options at the lowest market price.

Jenny: okay, what would be the flight charges and stay charges?

Joseph: Jenny, the flight charges for a return journey departing on the 15th and arriving on the 22nd would be $880, and staying in Holiday Inn for the same dates would be $2365 but that is the offer anyone doing online business will give you. Because we are official travel partners with both American

Airlines and Holiday Inn and we do bulk bookings with them in advance we can offer you the best price in the market.

Jenny: Well, that's great Joseph, what would be after discount prices?

Joseph: After our exclusive discount Jenny, the return flight tickets will become only $500, and the hotel stay will become only $1500. Also, this price includes free breakfast at the hotel throughout your stay. this is a special tailor-made offer just for you Jenny as you are working with us for the first time and this offer is valid only for this phone call.

Jenny: I am amazed Joseph. I have got quotations from almost five different companies but none comes even close to your offer price. I cannot miss this huge money-saving deal. I am glad I did not finalize the first deal I got, and kept searching the internet for better prices.

Joseph: You did the right thing, Jenny, please save our contact so that you don't have to do this whole search thing again on your next journey. To lock this exclusive deal please help me with your card details.

Jenny: Oh, okay. It's 4017-8596-6654-XXXX, expires 05/25, and the security code is 789.

Joseph: Thank you, Jenny, your flight is booked you must have gotten the debit message from the bank.

Jenny: yes, the debit message is received.

And that's how Jenny got scammed. But the scam doesn't stop here. As now scammer has her card details, they will try to charge it as much as possible to maximize the scam amount.

Red flags to look for in a flight booking scam:

Unsolicited Emails or Ads: Scammers often target individuals with unsolicited emails or advertisements claiming to offer exclusive or unrealistically cheap flight deals.

Too Good to Be True Discounts: Offers that seem too good to be true, such as extremely low prices or unrealistic discounts, should raise suspicion. Legitimate airlines typically have pricing structures within a certain range.

Unverified Contact Information: Lack of verifiable contact information for the airline, or discrepancies in contact details, can indicate a scam. Verify contact details directly from the official website of the airline.

Pressure Tactics and Urgency: Scammers create a sense of urgency, pressuring individuals to make quick decisions. They may claim limited availability or time-sensitive offers to encourage immediate action.

Request for Personal and Financial Information: Legitimate airlines do not request sensitive personal information, such as full addresses, passport details, or financial information, through unsolicited emails or ads.

Unsecured Websites: Ensure that the website where you are providing payment information is secure. Look for "https://" in the URL and a padlock icon in the address bar.

Fake Booking References: Scammers may provide fake booking references or confirmation numbers, making it difficult for victims to verify the authenticity of their reservations.

Unusual Payment Methods: Be cautious if the payment process involves unconventional methods or requires payment through untraceable channels, such as gift cards or wire transfers.

No Confirmation Email or Booking Details: Legitimate bookings are accompanied by official confirmation emails with detailed information about the flight. If you don't receive this, it may be a scam.

G. Social Media scam:

Social media scams come in various forms, including fake profiles, phishing links, and fraudulent ads. Scammers use social media platforms to impersonate trusted individuals or organizations and lure victims into sharing personal information or clicking on malicious links. These scams can result in identity theft, malware infections, and financial loss for unsuspecting users. Example:

Walmart is a very well-established and trusted brand. It has a presence on all big social media platforms where it engages with its customers and builds its community. If you visit any Walmart account on social media you will see some familiarities like the same logo and similar visual elements, it would also have similar color pallets and designs. The downside of this is it can be copied as well which can result in the creation of fake Walmart pages and profiles on social media.

One day Peter was scrolling through his Facebook feed and he stumbled upon a Walmart page named "Walmart clearance". It had the Walmart logo as a profile picture. He checks out the page and finds out that this page is dedicated to Walmart products that did not sell. Now Walmart has new products coming in and they have to get rid of the old products to clear inventory. To clear this stock quickly, Walmart is selling these products at a huge discount.

Peter gets really interested, and he sends a message to the admin of that page showing interest in a refrigerator. Just after a couple of minutes, he gets a reply on Facebook.

Sandra: thank you for showing interest in our product, could you specify what kind of refrigerator you are looking for?

Peter: I am looking for a side-by-side refrigerator with a capacity of 25 cu ft.

Sandra: I have a good option in stock for you. It is a Frigidaire Refrigerator, Black, Automatic Defrost FRSS2623AB. I am sending you the pictures now.

Peter: The product is looking great in the pictures. Can you tell me more about it?

Sandra: yes, I am sending you a link. It will take you to the Walmart website where this product is listed with detailed specifications and customer reviews. It will help you a lot.

Peter: Wow, it is really great and with the reviews, I can make out that people are loving this product. But $1043 is too much for me.

Sandra: well, I guess it is your lucky day, Peter. This product is available in stock clearance sale and it is the last piece we have. It is on discount.

Peter: how much?

Sandra: The actual product cost is $1043 + $159 is the shipping cost. It comes with two protection plans 3 years for $48 and 4 years for $89. So, the total would be around 1250-1300 depending upon which protection plan you take.

But as it is in clearance, this product is available only at $499 + $159 shipping, and 4 years of protection is complimentary from Walmart. This means that all the repair and hardware costs will be taken care of from our side If anything happens to this product in the next 4 years' time.

Peter: That's Amazing. I would love to have this kickass refrigerator in my house. But I would first like to visit and check this product.

Sandra: you are most welcome to do that sir but I am afraid that this unit will be sold till then. As there is more than 50%

off on this fridge, we are getting bulk inquiries. On top of that customers don't have to pay the price upfront, they only have to pay the shipping cost and once the product is shipped, you can pay the remaining cost at the time of delivery.

Peter: well, that makes more sense.

Sandra: I already have a customer here who is willing to pay, if you are not sure please let me know quickly, you inquired first that's why I am giving you first preference.

Peter: No wait. I can pay for shipping right now. When will be the product shipped?

Sandra: what is your zip code?

Peter: 859665

Sandra: it's not far, in the next 6 hours it will be at your door, sir.

Peter: Okay here is my card, you can charge it for $159. 4160-5898-8521-4736, 12/25, 058.

Sandra: I have charged it but it's not going through.

Peter: wait for 2 minutes, I have an extra protection on this card. My bank always calls me for authorization for any payment of more than $99.

Sandra: Well, I guess you have authorized it, it's done. Thank you for your payment. Your product is on the way and will be delivered in 5 to 6 hours.

Peter: Thank you, I will be waiting,

(After 4 hours Sandra calls him back)

Sandra: Hey Peter, we have a problem here.

Peter: What?

Sandra: While I was charging your payment, your bank took too long to authorize the transaction, and our discount page got timed out.

Peter: what do you mean by that?

Sandra: the discount page is timed for 60 seconds only, if the transaction doesn't get done in that time the page times out. My manager just told me about this issue. I am so sorry; I was not aware of that.

Peter: but now what? How do I get my fridge?

Sandra: We only have two options now, either you can pay the full price for the fridge or you can get me a Walmart card and I can re-apply this offer for you.

Peter: There is no way I am paying the full price. I will pay what I have promised you.

Sandra: well, I have a way to make this thing work. Do you have any Walmart stores near you?

Peter: Yes.

Sandra: Okay please head towards that store, sir. Your shipment is on the way. In how much time you will get there?

Peter: 10 minutes, but why?

Sandra: In this situation, the discount is not applied to your product. So, either you will have to pay the full price now or you can pay the promised amount at Walmart and get the fridge.

Peter: But it's your fault that you did not notify this thing at the time of the transaction. Talk to your manager and get it fixed from your side. I am not driving anywhere at this time.

Sandra: I am extremely sorry for that mistake sir. But if you don't go to Walmart, the product will not be shipped to you and the shipping cost of $159 will be lost which you paid around 4 hours ago.

Also, if my manager comes to know that it is my fault, they might take action against me or might fire me as well. In this dipping economy, they are just looking for reasons to fire people from their jobs. Please, I beg you sir to do this as I cannot risk my job at this point.

Peter: okay, I don't want to be a trouble for you. I will do it but you better not do this again with anyone.

Sandra: Thank you so much, sir. It means a lot to me. As a token of gratitude, I am giving you an additional $9 off. Now instead of $499 you only have to pay $490 at the Walmart store.

Peter: Okay that's nice, I am at the store where do I pay?

Sandra: just grab a Walmart money card and load It with $490 once you have it let me know.

Peter: ok.

Peter (after 5 minutes): I have the card.

Sandra: ok, just scratch the back of the card and give me the numbers at the back.

Peter: 5269-8524-7895-3265 Pin: 4582.

And that's how Peter got scammed. Here he got scammed twice, first with $159 and then with $490 and it may not be the last payment scammers demand. They can come up with numerous more reasons to charge more.

Red flags to look out for in social media scams:

Too Good to Be True Offers: Be skeptical of posts or messages promising unbelievable deals, prizes, or giveaways. Scammers often use enticing offers to lure victims.

Urgent or Threatening Messages: Scammers may create a sense of urgency by claiming your account is compromised or that immediate action is required. Scammers can also create urgency by claiming that this too-good-to-be-true offer is valid only for the next 10 or 15 minutes. Avoid clicking on links or providing information in response to urgent messages.

Fake Profiles or Impersonation: Watch out for fake profiles impersonating well-known individuals, celebrities, or companies. Verify the authenticity of accounts by checking for verification badges or contacting the entity directly.

H. Online Shopping Scam:

Online shopping scams involve fraudulent websites or sellers offering products at unrealistically low prices. Victims may place orders and make payments, only to receive counterfeit or never receive any products. These scams exploit the convenience of online shopping and can leave victims with substandard or nonexistent goods. Example:

Henry is searching for Air Jordans online. He came across many websites but the prices were too high. Henry doesn't give up hope and keeps his search active believing somewhere he will get them at an affordable price. He keeps searching in the hope of some big sale or the right offer. After a couple of days, he finds a website "Luxegadgets.com". It is a marketplace dedicated to sneakers where people can buy and sell sneakers. The sellers list their products on the website and buyers bid for them. On that website, Henery finds the Air Jordan he was looking for at an unbelievable price. It was listed by a person named Logan. He messages Logan on the website to buy the product.

Henry: Hi, I am interested in the Jordans that you are selling.

Logan: that's great. I want to sell them ASAP.

Henry: I have been searching for these pairs for the last two weeks but never found them at this price.

Logan: these pairs are my love. I have had them for the last four years but I have only worn them once when I bought them and since then I have kept them in a showcase in my drawing room as my priced possession.

Henry: These are really good shoes with a great story. Why are you selling them and that too at a very low price?

Logan: I never thought that I would ever sell them. But my brother is in the hospital. Yesterday he suffered a road accident and is currently under treatment. I need the funds urgently.

Henry: Oh. That's sad.

Logan: Yes, it is but I can tell you one thing, these pairs are worth buying. If you buy them, I can ship them to you ASAP and it will be a big help for me as well as I will get funds to pay the hospital bills.

Henry: I really want to buy the shoes and I will really feel good if I can help you here.

Logan: My cash app ID is $Logan2568. You can send me the payment and the shipping address.

Henry: I want to help you but I will pay once I receive the product.

Logan: I am sorry my friend but I am selling these shoes at a 60% discount only because I need the funds urgently. If you go to the market, these are for $1000. I am selling at $400 because I need the funds immediately.

Henry: yes, I am totally aware of that. But there are a lot of scams going on and I want to protect my money.

Logan: The website you have visited is 100% legit. I have done my verification here. My ID, my address everything is been verified. there is no scope of doubt here. Instead, I should doubt you because I can see that you have an unverified account.

Henry: this is the first time I have visited this website. That is why my account is showing unverified.

Logan: I should be doubting you here but I don't have time to waste here. You can do one thing. You can pay half the money now and you can pay half the money after receiving the shoes.

Henry: Well, that sounds fair to me.

Logan: $Logan2568 send $200 on this cash app ID and send me a screenshot.

Henry: it is done.

And yes, you thought right. That's how Henry got scammed.

Red flags to look out for in online shopping scams:

Too Good to Be True Deals: Extremely low prices or discounts that seem unrealistic for the product or brand.

Unsecure Website: Check for "https://" in the URL and a padlock symbol in the address bar. Avoid entering personal information on websites without these security features.

Poor Website Design: Grammatical errors, spelling mistakes, or poorly designed websites may indicate a lack of professionalism and could be a sign of a scam.

No Contact Information: Legitimate online stores provide clear contact information, including a physical address and customer support. Be wary if this information is missing or difficult to find.

Limited Payment Options: Scammers may restrict payment options to wire transfers, money orders, or unconventional methods. Legitimate sites usually offer a variety of secure payment options.

Fake Customer Reviews: Check for reviews on third-party websites or platforms, as fake reviews or the absence of reviews on the seller's site can be suspicious.

Unusual Requests for Personal Information: Be cautious if a website asks for excessive personal information or information that seems unnecessary for the transaction.

No Return Policy or Unclear Terms: Legitimate sellers have clear return policies and terms of service. Be wary if this information is missing or difficult to understand.

Pressure Tactics: Scammers may use high-pressure tactics to rush you into making a purchase. Be skeptical of countdown timers or limited availability claims.

Lack of Verifiable Contact Information: Check for a valid phone number and email address. If the only means of communication is through a web form, be cautious.

6. The scam protection system:

Till now we have analyzed a lot of scams. We have explored 8 categories and 15 subcategories of scams and we have also covered pointers to detect them and protect from them. Have we covered all the scams present online? The answer is NO.

It is practically not possible to cover all the scams in one book as it is a rapidly evolving field. Technological changes reflect in scams. At present when I am writing this book, there are a lot of developments happening in the field of Artificial Intelligence. Scammers and social engineers may start using AI as a tool to make their scams more realistic and effective. It is also highly possible that they might discover a new loophole or come up with a new concept that was never heard of before. They may start new operations impersonating Better Business Bureau or Transportation Security Administration (TSA).

The possibilities of modifications, alterations, and innovation of scam processes are very high, which is why it is not possible to list them all in one book. But the method that I am going to discuss now can surely give you a huge advantage over scammers. After doing hours of research on the internet I couldn't find a simple system that people can remember at their fingertips and execute when required. So, I created a method keeping simplicity in mind. I firmly believe that for effective execution of an idea it needs to be extremely simple. So, if you felt earlier in this book that the steps mentioned to detect and prevent fraud were too much to remember and difficult to execute here is a simple method created by me to help you examine, detect, and prevent fraud.

Step 1: Test the Trust: If you get a call, email, or text message from a brand you use, a person you know, or a government organization asking you to do something. Always test their trust factor and authenticity. Reputed organizations have SOPs (Standard operating procedures) in place and a system to do everything. For example, if Microsoft wants to warn you about something and you ask them to send you an email, they will never refuse. If the IRS wants to take action against you for not paying taxes, they will first send you something in black and white informing you about the discrepancies.

So, if someone is trying to establish trust with you, put it to the test by asking for information from the right means of communication. Ask for a callback number, reach out for help from an expert, and check and scan their website. Instead of simply trusting what they are saying, ask for written communication and proof.

Step 2: Tickle the Trigger: Remember the spell "Riddikulus" from Harry Potter. Whenever the young magicians felt fear of boggart, they turned them into funny things using this spell. Converting your fears into humor is literally magical because it helps you to think better leading you to make better decisions. While facing a scam call, scammers will always use harsh tactics to bait you with fear or greed. In that moment don't lose your sense of humor as it keeps your rational mind active.

If the brain gets triggered into fear or greed it will start feeling things instead of understanding things and that is exactly what the scammers want. Humor will keep your rational mind active and you will start responding to the situation instead of reacting. Remember the difference, Reacting is an instinctive, emotional response to a situation. It's often impulsive and can be influenced by our past experiences or fears.

On the other hand, responding is a thoughtful and deliberate action. It involves considering the situation, weighing the options, and making a conscious decision. So, whenever faced with fear never react, always respond.

Step 3: Unarm the Urgency: As you have experienced in the 15 examples covered in this book, there is always urgency to make the payment. Sometimes it is to resolve the matter, to fix the device, to sell the product, or a limited-time offer. By creating urgency, scammers want you to act immediately, eliminating your options to think clearly and make rational decisions. When you act in a hurry you give a lot of control to the scammer. Instead, you should always keep control and analyze the intentions behind the instructions given to you.

Now let us remove the time factor from this situation. Imagine instead a time limit of 30 mins or 60 mins, you have the whole day to act on this matter. You can re-examine the whole situation, you can ask as many questions as you want, and you can think it through without the time pressure. How much better decisions you can make, if you don't have the fear of that ticking clock? The urgency created by the scammers of the ticking clock is like a ticking time bomb for you. But remember that you are the one in control and you can disarm it whenever you want. Stay relaxed, stay in control, and don't rush into decision-making.

Step 4: Solve the Secrecy: Keep the matter private and confidential. Do not tell the storekeeper. Do not tell the bank teller. You cannot involve your friends and family in this matter. These are some common lines you will hear in scam calls. Whenever you hear these lines ask questions to solve this secrecy.

The opinions of friends and family are always important. We value them in the most important decisions of our life, like choosing a school or college, deciding on a career path or even choosing our life partner. Secrecy steals away the support system we have around us and that makes us weak and vulnerable. If you feel something fishy do not hesitate to ask for advice from your friends and family. You can also take advice from a subject matter expert like a lawyer, sheriff, police officer, local technician, IT person etcetera. People around us are very important. Do not let the scammers take them away from you in your weak moments. Talk to them, ask for advice, and share the incident.

Step 5: Lock the loopholes: You need to buy a Target gift card, Walmart gift card, eBay, Sephora, or any other gift card to make this payment. You need to go and put money into a Bitcoin machine. You need to make a wire transfer to secure your funds. You need to send a cash app payment. Just think about it. Reputed Organizations such as the IRS, Microsoft, Amazon, SSA, and many more are respected not only in the USA but in the whole world, why would they take payments from gift cards or crypto? These companies have the talent, resources, and finances to develop their own payment system which can run parallel to other payment systems which already exist. Why would they rely on gift cards and cryptocurrencies which are highly skeptical? The truth is they don't. they will always provide you with a payment option that is trusted and authentic.

So, if someone impersonating these big companies asks for payments in gift cards and cryptocurrencies, they are just trying to exploit a loophole in the payment system. Because these modes of payments are easily redeemable for the scammers and are either untraceable or very difficult to trace. Whenever you get asked for these kinds of payment methods just refuse and lock that loophole.

Dear reader, next time if you face a scam situation and your mind becomes numb and you don't know what to do next just remember this five-step process:

Test the trust -> Tickle the trigger -> Unarm the urgency -> Solve the secrecy-> Lock the loophole.

This easy method will protect you from multiple kinds of scams. In case it gets blurry in your memory, just go through this chapter again and you will be confident and equipped to disarm any scam situation.

7. A solution to this five-decade-old problem?

The genesis of online scams traces back to the 1970s, marked by an early phishing attack, setting the stage for an unfortunate trend that has only intensified over the years. Despite the passage of more than five decades, we might expect increased awareness and resilience among individuals. But, the number of victims continues to rise annually. This alarming trend is a result of our collective failure to prioritize education and upskilling against the ever-advancing tactics employed by scammers.

Our busy lives have inadvertently become a breeding ground for scams, with scammers leveraging technology and social engineering to refine and amplify their attacks. The excessive number of online articles offering advice on scam protection often fail to save people from getting scammed because of three major reasons.

> Firstly, the knowledge acquired from these articles tends to fade over time, leaving individuals ill-equipped when faced with a potential scam.
>
> Secondly, the perfect-sounding advice on paper may prove challenging to execute in the heat of a scam attack.
>
> Lastly, the rapidly evolving nature of the tech world leaves much of the knowledge obsolete and irrelevant just in a couple of months.

To combat this frustrating problem that drains you both mentally and financially I have created a solution. As you must have heard, doctors don't make you healthy, fitness trainers don't make you fit, and business coaches don't make you rich. They just show you the path. It is your continuous efforts that eventually make you healthy, fit, and, rich. Similarly, the solution to this fifty-year-old problem is continuous learning. Here, Continuous learning does not mean that you shell out multiple hours every week to learn something instead just a simple newsletter that gets delivered to your inbox once a week and a swift 5-minute read that equips you with all the updates to combat scam situations.

To register yourself for this super informative newsletter that makes you scam proof just send an email to info@thescamprotector.com and we will send you the invite. Please note that our official domain is www.thescamprotector.com and our official email is info@thescamprotector.com. Anything apart from this like "scamprotector.com", "thescamprotector.org", "scamprotector.co", or anything else is a domain spoofing version and is not a part of our community. So, always check the spelling first. If it is not from www.thescamprotector.com or info@thescamprotector.com it is not from us and can be fake or scam.

I also want to inform you through this book that **we do not have a Facebook page, Instagram page, telegram group, WhatsApp group, or any other group or profile. We will only communicate with you through our official email address** which is info@thescamprotector.com. DO NOT ENTERTAIN ANY COMMUNICATION APART FROM THIS EMAIL ADDRESS.

8. Join the revolution

Dear readers,

If you resonate with the idea of a scam-free society where people are educated about scams, where billions of dollars are not lost annually to fraudsters, and where individuals do not feel driven towards suicide due to the embarrassment and devastation caused by scams, then I invite you to join me on a revolutionary journey.

The prevalence of online scams has reached epidemic proportions, infiltering our digital lives and preying on innocent people with increasing sophistication and frequency. From phishing emails and fake websites to identity theft and investment scams, the tactics used by fraudsters are as diverse as they are damaging.

But what if we could change that? What if we could harness the power of collective action to put an end to the curse of online scams once and for all? That's precisely what I am proposing—a bold and audacious revolution to reclaim our digital world from the clutches of scammers and fraudsters.

Imagine a world where every person is armed with the knowledge and resources to identify and prevent scams before they can harm. Picture a society where individuals are empowered to protect themselves and their loved ones from falling victim to fraudulent schemes. Envision a future where trust, transparency, and integrity reign supreme in our online interactions.

To kickstart this revolution, I have launched "The Scam Protector," a comprehensive guidebook designed to educate and empower individuals to recognize, avoid, and combat online scams. This book is not just a tool for self-defense—it is a manifesto for change, a call to arms for all those who refuse to be victims of deception and manipulation.

But I cannot do this alone. I need your help to spread the word and enlist others in our fight against online scams. I urge you to share this book with your friends, family, and relatives, and encourage them to join our movement. Together, we can amplify our impact and reach even more people with the knowledge and tools they need to protect themselves from scams. I also urge you to share your honest feedback about this book, so that I can make improvements to this book and make it more effective.

In addition to sharing the book, I invite you to register yourself on the thescamprotector newsletter program by sending an email to info@thescamprotector.com There are so many dark secrets of the online scam industry and additional resources that cannot be shared in this book. The registration will also help you to access additional resources, connect with fellow members, and stay updated on the latest developments in our fight against online scams.

Together, let us embark on this revolutionary journey to create a safer, more secure digital world for ourselves and our future generations. The time for action is now, and the power to make a difference lies within each and every one of us. If you feel that this book has added value to your life and made you feel more confident against the scammers then take action on these three steps to spread this revolution:

- Leave a review on the marketplace from where you purchased this book.
- Refer this book to at least three people, who you think need this book the most.
- Send an email to **info@thescamprotector.com** And gain access to our exclusive content via our newsletter.

My sincere thanks and gratitude to all the readers for investing their time, money, and attention in this book.

Acknowledgments

I would like to express my sincere gratitude to the following individuals and organizations whose support and contributions made "The Scam Protector" possible:

- Gloria Hunniford, for her insightful work in "The Little Book of Big Scams," which served as inspiration and a valuable resource in the creation of this book.

- The Federal Trade Commission website, for providing extensive data and information on online scams, which greatly informed the content of this book.

- Perplexity and Google Search engine, for their invaluable role in conducting research and gathering relevant information for the development of this book.

- My supportive family, whose unwavering encouragement and understanding throughout the writing process were instrumental in bringing this project to fruition.

- Last but not least, to my loving wife, whose endless patience, encouragement, and support made it possible for me to dedicate the time and effort needed to complete this book. Your love and belief in me were the driving forces behind this endeavor.

Thank you all for your invaluable contributions and for being a part of this important cause to protect individuals from online scams.

About the author

Hi everyone, now it is time that you know me. As a reader, it is your right to know why I am writing this book and what makes me qualified to provide you with knowledge on scam protection.

You would be surprised to know that this book is a feel-good and karma-cleansing exercise for me. I am not a saint who is 100% pure. I have had my fair share of sin. I was in college when I discovered that my family had huge loans on them. I did not know that they were drowning in a debt trap until one day when I was stopped from attending classes in college due to unpaid college fees. I had to quit my studies and to pay off the debt I had to start doing odd jobs as well. After working multiple underpaying jobs that were exploiting my compulsion, I finally got a decent-paying job in a BPO. At the time of the interview, I was told that I would be working as a customer support executive for a Microsoft affiliate company and I was at the peak of my excitement. After a week of working there, I realized that they lied to me and it was a tech support company that was scamming people. I felt cheated but I stayed.

In the early days, it was all fun and money was good. We used to celebrate every time we used to con someone. It used to feel like we were super smart. I was outstanding in my communication and repo building with victims and that's all that mattered in that job. I started becoming big in the industry and soon I started trying my hands at bigger scams like IRS, SSN etcetera. I paid off my family's debt but, a lot changed inside me.

Ticket sizes in tech support scams were small like $200-$500. If we used to take the money, we also used to provide some services on victims' computers like boosting up speed, setting up email and search engines, Facebook and email login issues, and any other thing victims needed help with. It doesn't used to feel like a scam but like selling services at expensive rates. Victims rarely used to abuse us, they never cried on the phone in tech support scams, sometimes we used to do services for free also when the victim didn't have money to pay. But in government-imposters scams things were different. I heard people cry on the phone begging us not to arrest them. Ticket sizes in these scams had no limits. It can go from $100 to $100,000 or maybe $1,000,000. Where I used to enjoy my tech support job I started hating every single day of my government imposter job, I wanted to quit but I knew that I needed the money, and if I quit, I wouldn't have the qualifications to obtain a job that can pay me that much. Even though I managed to pay off my family's debts, I felt guilty and lost. So, I tried my hand at starting some honest businesses, but things didn't go well and I failed miserably in four businesses.

I lost hope and created a shell for myself. I stopped going out and stopped meeting people. I did not know what to do with my life until one day I saw a short on YouTube that was trying to spread awareness about online scams. The comments on that short were extremely positive, they were literally like blessings from people. It was like "god bless you", "Thank you for telling this to us. More power to you" and many more. Reading those comments from people torched a spark inside me. At that moment, I felt like I knew what I wanted to do and I could do it better than most of the people out there. I started finding content and books on the internet but I did not find a single book or article that exactly described real-life scam scenarios, scam psychology, and protection tips that can be executed in the heat of a scam situation. This problem turned me into a scam analyst and then into an author. I have worked very hard in compiling the contents of this book in such a way that it can be relatable and understandable.

When I started this book, I had no experience in writing. I never imagined in the wildest of my dreams that writing could be such a Herculean task. I wanted to finish this book in a month but it took four. But I am happy that with the release of this book, I was able to accomplish the first step of my mission. If the contents of this book can save even a single person from getting scammed, it would be a great success for me. I once again express my deepest gratitude and thank you for investing in this book and completing it.

Adam
The Scam Protector.

Manufactured by Amazon.ca
Bolton, ON